Primary SPACE Project Research Team

Research Co-ordinating Group

Professor Paul Black (Co-director)
Jonathan Osborne

Dr Wynne Harlen (Co-director)
Terry Russell

Centre for Educational Studies
King's College London
University of London
Cornwall House Annexe
Waterloo Road
London SE1 8TZ

Centre for Research in Primary Science
  and Technology
Department of Education
University of Liverpool
126 Mount Pleasant
Liverpool L3 5SR

Tel: 071 872 3094

Tel: 051 794 3270

Project Researchers

Pamela Wadsworth (from 1989)

Derek Bell (from 1989)
Ken Longden (from 1989)
Adrian Hughes (1989)
Linda McGuigan (from 1989)
Dorothy Watt (1986-89)

Associated Researchers

John Meadows
(South Bank Polytechnic)

Bert Sorsby
John Entwistle
(Edge Hill College)

LEA Advisory Teachers

Maureen Smith (1986-89)
(ILEA)

Joan Boden
Karen Hartley
Kevin Cooney (1986-88)
(Knowsley)

Joyce Knaggs (1986-88)
Heather Scott (from 1989)
Ruth Morton (from 1989)
(Lancashire)

PRIMARY SPACE PROJECT
RESEARCH REPORT
January 1990

Growth

by
TERRY RUSSELL and DOROTHY WATT

LIVERPOOL UNIVERSITY PRESS

First published 1990 by
Liverpool University Press
PO Box 147, Liverpool L69 3BX

Reprinted, with corrections, 1992

British Library Cataloguing in Publication Data
Data are available
ISBN 0 85323 476 0

Printed and bound by
Antony Rowe Limited, Chippenham, England

CONTENTS

INTRODUCTION

The Primary SPACE Project is a classroom-based research project which aims to establish

     .   *the ideas which primary school children have in particular science concept areas*

     .   *the possibility of children modifying their ideas as the result of relevant experiences.*

The research reported here was funded by the Nuffield Foundation and is being conducted at two centres, the Centre for Research in Primary Science and Technology, Department of Education, University of Liverpool and the Centre for Educational Studies, King's College, London. The joint directors are Professor Wynne Harlen and Professor Paul Black. Three local education authorities are involved: Inner London Education Authority, Knowsley and Lancashire.

The Project is based on the view that children develop their ideas through the experiences they have. With this in mind, the Project has two main aims: firstly, to establish (through an elicitation phase) what specific ideas children have developed and what experiences might have led children to hold these views; and secondly, to see whether, within a normal classroom environment, it is possible to encourage a change in the ideas in a direction which will help children develop a more 'scientific' understanding of the topic (the intervention phase).

The concept areas studied so far have included:

> *Electricity*
> *Evaporation and condensation*
> *Everyday changes in non-living materials*
> *Forces and their effect on movement*
> *Growth*
> *Light*
> *Living things' sensitivity to their environment*
> *Sound.*

The Project has been run collaboratively between the University research teams, local education authorities and schools, with the participating teachers playing an active role in the development of the Project work.

A close relationship has been established between the University researchers and the teachers, resulting in the development of techniques which advance both classroom practice and research. These methods provide opportunities, within the classroom, for children to express their ideas and to develop their thinking with the guidance of the teacher, and also help researchers towards a better understanding of children's thinking.

The involvement of teachers

Schools and teachers were not selected for the Project on the basis of a particular background or expertise in primary science. In the majority of cases, two teachers per school were involved, which was advantageous in providing mutual support. Where possible, the Authority provided supply cover for the teachers so that they could attend Project sessions for preparation, training and discussion, during the school day. Sessions were also held in the teachers' own time, after school.

The Project team aimed to have as much contact as possible with the teachers throughout the work to facilitate the provision of both training and support. The diversity of experience and differences in teaching style which the teachers brought with them to the Project meant that achieving a uniform style of presentation in all classrooms would not have been possible, or even desirable. Teachers were encouraged to incorporate the Project work into their existing classroom organisation so that both they and the children were as much at ease with the work as with any other classroom experience.

The involvement of children

The Project involved a cross-section of classes of children throughout the primary age range. A large component of the Project work was classroom-based, and all of the children in the participating classes were involved as far as possible. Small groups of children and individuals were selected for additional activities or interviews to facilitate more detailed discussion of their thinking.

The structure of the Project

For each of the eight concept areas studied, a list of concepts was compiled to be used by researchers as the basis for the development of work in that area. These lists were drawn up from the standpoint of accepted scientific understanding and contained concepts which were considered to be a necessary part of a scientific understanding of each topic. The lists were not necessarily considered to be statements of the understanding which would be desirable in a child at age eleven, at the end of the Primary phase of schooling. The concept lists defined and outlined the area of interest for each of the studies; what ideas children were able to develop was a matter for empirical investigation.

Most of the Project research work can be regarded as being organised into four phases, preceded by an extensive pilot phase. These phases are described in the following paragraphs and were as follows:

Pilot work
Phase 1: Exploration
Phase 2: Pre-Intervention Elicitation
Phase 3: Intervention
Phase 4: Post-Intervention Elicitation

The phases of the research

Each phase, particularly the Pilot work, was regarded as developmental; techniques and procedures were modified in the light of experience. The modifications involved a refinement of both the exposure materials and the techniques used to elicit ideas. This flexibility allowed the Project team to respond to unexpected situations and to incorporate useful developments into the programme.

There were three main aims of the Pilot phase. Firstly, to trial the techniques used to establish children's ideas; secondly, to establish the range of ideas held by primary school children; and thirdly, to familiarise the teachers with the classroom techniques being employed by the Project. This third aim was very important since teachers were being asked to operate in a manner which, to many of them, was very different from their usual style. By allowing teachers a 'practice run', their initial apprehensions were reduced, and the Project rationale became more familiar. In other words, teachers were being given the opportunity to incorporate Project techniques into their teaching, rather than having them imposed upon them.

In the Exploration phase children engaged with activities set up in the classroom for them to use, without any direct teaching. The activities were designed to ensure that a range of fairly common experiences (with which children might well be familiar from their everyday lives) was uniformly accessible to all children to provide a focus for their thoughts. In this way, the classroom activities were to help children articulate existing ideas rather than to provide them with novel experiences which would need to be interpreted.

Each of the topics studied raised some unique issues of technique and these distinctions led to the Exploration phase receiving differential emphasis. Topics in which the central concepts involved long-term, gradual changes, e.g. 'Growth', necessitated the incorporation of a lengthy exposure period in the study. A much shorter period of exposure, directly prior to elicitation was used with 'Light' and 'Electricity', two topics involving 'instant' changes.

During the Exploration, teachers were encouraged to collect their children's ideas using informal classroom techniques. These techniques were:

i. *Using log-books (free writing/drawing)*

Where the concept area involved long-term changes, it was suggested that children should make regular observations of the materials, with the frequency of these depending on the rate of change. The log-books could be pictorial or written, depending on the age of the children involved, and any entries could be supplemented by teacher comment if the children's thoughts needed explaining more fully. The main purposes of these log-books were to focus attention on the activities and to provide an informal record of the children's observations and ideas.

ii. *Structured writing/drawing*

Writing or drawings produced in response to a particular question were extremely informative. This was particularly so when the teacher asked children to clarify their diagrams and themselves added explanatory notes and comments where necessary, after seeking clarification from children.

Teachers were encouraged to note down any comments which emerged during dialogue, rather than ask children to write them down themselves. It was felt that this technique would remove a pressure from children which might otherwise have inhibited the expression of their thoughts.

iii. *Completing a picture*

Children were asked to add the relevant points to a picture. This technique ensured that children answered the question posed by the Project team and reduced the possible effects of competence in drawing skills on ease of expression of ideas. The structured drawing provided valuable opportunities for teachers to talk to individual children and to build up a picture of each child's understanding.

iv. *Individual discussion*

It was suggested that teachers use an open-ended questioning style with their children. The value of listening to what children said, and of respecting their responses, was emphasised as was the importance of clarifying the meaning of words children used. This style of questioning caused some teachers to be concerned that, by accepting any response whether right or wrong, they might implicitly be reinforcing incorrect ideas. The notion of ideas being acceptable and yet provisional until tested was at the heart of the Project. Where this philosophy was a novelty, some conflict was understandable.

In the Elicitation phase, the Project team collected structured data through individual interviews and work with small groups. The individual interviews were held with a random, stratified sample of children to establish the frequencies of ideas held. The same sample of children was interviewed pre- and post-Intervention so that any shifts in ideas could be identified.

The Elicitation phase produced a wealth of different ideas from children, and led to some tentative insights into experiences which could have led to the genesis of some of these ideas. During the Intervention teachers used this information as a starting point for classroom activities, or interventions, which were intended to lead to children extending their ideas. In schools where a significant level of teacher involvement was possible, teachers were provided with a general framework to guide their structuring of classroom activities appropriate to their class. Where opportunities for exposing teachers to Project techniques were more limited, teachers were given a package of activities which had been developed by the Project team.

Both the framework and the intervention activities were developed as a result of preliminary analysis of the Pre-Intervention Elicitation data. The Intervention strategies were:

(a) Encouraging children to test their ideas

It was felt that, if pupils were provided with the opportunity to test their ideas in a scientific way, they might find some of their ideas to be unsatisfying. This might encourage the children to develop their thinking in a way compatible with greater scientific competence.

(b) Encouraging children to develop more specific definitions for particular key words

Teachers asked children to make collections of objects which exemplified particular words, thus enabling children to define words in a relevant context, through using them.

(c) Encouraging children to generalise from one specific context to others through discussion.

Many ideas which children held appeared to be context-specific. Teachers provided children with opportunities to share ideas and experiences so that they might be enabled to broaden the range of contexts in which their ideas applied.

(d) Finding ways to make imperceptible changes perceptible

Long-term, gradual changes in objects which could not readily be perceived were problematic for many children. Teachers endeavoured to find appropriate ways of making these changes perceptible. For example, the fact that a liquid could 'disappear' visually and yet still be sensed by the sense of smell - as in the case of perfume - might make the concept of evaporation more accessible to children.

(e) Testing the 'right' idea alongside the children's own ideas

Children were given activities which involved solving a problem. To complete the activity, a scientific idea had to be applied correctly, thus challenging the child's notion. This confrontation might help children to develop a more scientific idea.

In the Post-Intervention Elicitation phase the Project team collected a complementary set of data to that from the Pre-Intervention Elicitation by re-interviewing the same sample of children. The data were analysed to identify changes in ideas across the sample as a whole and also in individual children.

These four phases of Project work form a coherent package which provides opportunities for children to explore and develop their scientific understanding as a part of classroom activity, and enables researchers to come nearer to establishing what conceptual development it is possible to encourage within the classroom and the most effective strategies for its encouragement.

The implications of the research

The SPACE Project has developed a programme which has raised many issues in addition to those of identifying and changing children's ideas in a classroom context. The question of teacher and pupil involvement in such work has become an important part of the Project, and the acknowledgement of the complex interactions inherent in the classroom has led to findings which report changes in teacher and pupil attitudes as well as in ideas. Consequently, the central core of activity, with its pre- and post-test design, should be viewed as just one of the several kinds of change upon which the efficacy of the Project must be judged.

The following pages provide a detailed account of the development of the Growth topic, the Project findings and the implications which they raise for science education.

1. METHODOLOGY

1.1 SAMPLE

The six participating schools belonged to Lancashire LEA, and were situated in or around Preston. Five of them were primary, the sixth being a junior school. The classes included in the sample covered the whole primary range, from rising-five to eleven. At some stage in the Project there had been two teachers involved from each school, though one teacher joined late and another had been absent due to ill health. Names of schools, Head Teachers and teachers are in Appendix I.

Teachers

Teachers were able to receive support visits from an advisory teacher who was closely involved in the project and liaised between the schools and the University as 'Growth' group co-ordinator. These visits served the purposes of boosting morale and providing an extra pair of hands in the classroom on occasions. The relationship which already existed between the teachers and advisory teacher was advantageous to the project since it enabled teachers to express any lack of confidence and gain clarification or help more easily than directly from the research team.

Children

A stratified random sample of children from the target classes was selected to be interviewed by members of the project team at stages during the work. Initially, children's ideas were informally surveyed, and teacher opinion sought in order that interviews might be conducted with children who had clearly expressed ideas. In this way, the research team had access to a very wide range of ideas held by children. With this range established, and prior to the more structured interviews, teachers were asked to assign each child in their class to an achievement band (high, middle or low) related to their overall school performance. Children were then randomly selected from the class list so that numbers were balanced by achievement band and sex. Data from these interviews provided quantitative information about the frequency and distribution of ideas.

1.2 THE RESEARCH PROGRAMME

Classroom work concerning 'Growth' took place during three periods of the school year. Each of these phases was followed by interviewing to establish the ideas of a sample of the children in participating classes. The phases were :

Pilot (March 1987)

Pilot Elicitation (April 1987)

Exploration (October 1987)

Pre-Intervention Elicitation (October 1987)

Intervention (November 1987)

Post-Intervention Elicitation (January 1988)

1.3 DEFINING 'GROWTH'

The following list of concepts concerning growth was compiled to be used as an orientation for the work in this area:

1. Everything which is living has the ability to grow.

2. Growth requires energy which is provided by food.

    - plants make their own food from raw materials

    - animals eat ready-made food

3. The food materials are transformed and incorporated into structural material.

4. The mass, volume and shape of the organism change as a result of growth.

5. Each organism has an optimum size to which it grows (in favourable conditions).

6. Growth takes time to happen, and this time varies with conditions and between organisms.

2. ACTIVITIES PRIOR TO INTERVENTION

2.1 PILOT ACTIVITIES

As one of the first topics to be researched within the Primary SPACE Project programme, the work on 'Growth' was preceded by a fairly extensive pilot phase. The pilot phase enabled the researchers to refine procedures in the light of exposure to classroom conditions as well as to gain some broad insights into the kind of information which it might be possible to collect. The pilot phase also gave the participating teachers time and opportunity to clarify their own roles by discovering what was viable and useful for them. Because of its importance, the pilot phase is reported in some detail in the first part of this section. The guidelines provided for teachers, the exploration activities and the elicitation techniques are all described. The second part of this section describes the refined activities as they were deployed in the study proper. The quantified data presented in later sections is based on these latter activities and techniques.

The Pilot phase activities to which children were exposed were as follows:

a sprouting potato tuber

a sprouting carrot top

germinating mung beans

maize seeds grown in soil

maize seeds grown in water

broad beans grown in water

monitoring stick insect's growth

incubating hens' eggs

children measuring their own height and weight

These activities were chosen with particular criteria in mind: it was important that the materials would grow reliably and that the amount of growth over the three week period prior to interviewing would be sufficient to be appreciated and measured by the children. Stick insects, while maybe not very widely experienced by the children previously, would grow about two centimetres during that time and might shed a skin as well. The mung beans were soaked, drained and placed in a jar in a dark cupboard. The broad beans were grown on trays of damp cotton wool. This was to enable the root growth to be observed more easily. These species of seed were chosen for their relatively short germination period, and for their rapid development. Potato tubers and hens' eggs were included as examples of growth which is relatively 'self-contained' and would proceed without the addition of extraneous materials, given suitable conditions.

The activities were set up in the classroom for a period of five weeks, during which time teachers were asked to encourage their children to observe the activities carefully. The teachers were each visited by the group co-ordinator and research co-ordinator during this period to iron out any difficulties with materials or procedures.

Teacher Guidelines

Teachers were provided with guidelines about how to set up the activities, and how to introduce them to their classes. These guidelines contained lists of equipment, details of preparation of the activities including germination times, suggestions for methods of recording the children's ideas and observations, and possible questions to ask the children about the activities. The guidelines may be found in Appendix II.

Teachers were asked to make the activities accessible to children in their classrooms and to encourage the class to take an interest in them, without actually teaching the children anything about them. It was suggested that the activities might be introduced in terms such as:

> "Here are some things we're going to have around in the classroom. Have
> a careful look at them every now and again and make a note of anything
> that's changed."

The growing materials all changed gradually over the period they were in the classroom and were not incorporated into any classroom work that the teachers were undertaking.

Classroom Implementation of the Activities

The teacher guidelines were interpreted and put into practice in slightly different ways, from teacher to teacher. This was in keeping with the policy of encouraging teachers to incorporate project work into their normal teaching style, and it did not effect the range of experiences which was available to each child. The efficacy of particular activities varied to some extent from class to class and from one age group to another, as did the different techniques for finding out the children's ideas. The brief outline which follows summarises the reactions to the activities and methods of elicitation.

Activities

Sprouting potato tuber

■

This was the only activity to be mishandled by the children. In several classes children removed the shoots and roots from the potatoes (perhaps inadvertently, due to rough handling) as soon as they sprouted, making them very uninteresting. Even where this did not happen the potato evoked little interest - except in one class, where children appeared to be fascinated by its growth.

Sprouting carrot top

■

These proved unreliable as they often failed to sprout. Those carrot tops which did sprout leaves did not produce roots.

Germinating mung beans

■

The mung beans proved to be interesting for the children: they changed noticeably in both size and colour when they were soaked in water, and on germination both root and shoot were clearly visible after a comparatively short time. These were grown successfully by all teachers, though sometimes two attempts were necessary. The main problem was that the beans had to be rinsed every day and then drained of water; if any water was left with the beans they tended to start rotting and smelling.

Maize seeds grown in soil

■

Maize was selected for its rapid, straight growth. Unfortunately, it did not germinate very well in a classroom environment, perhaps as the result of low temperatures.

Maize seeds grown in water

■

Germination was very slow, and the swelling of the seed in water did not tend to be as noticeable as with other seeds.

Broad beans grown in water

■

These swelled noticeably on soaking and germinated well though they tended to dry out with the shoot often going black. Once well established, the growth of both shoot and roots was sufficient to hold children's interest.

Monitoring stick insect's growth

■

The stick insects were immediately interesting for the children to watch, even though they moved very little. Unfortunately the stick insects, an ideal shape for measuring, invariably started moving very fast whenever children tried to measure them. This diversion proved to be time-consuming and rather frustrating. Most of the stick insects moulted at least once, providing another tangible, if puzzling, piece of evidence of growth occurring.

Incubating hens' eggs

■

This activity generated the most excitement and interest. The care of an incubator full of eggs was demanding for the teachers, but the value to the children of watching the eggs hatch was considered to be so great that the anxieties were forgotten. Every teacher except one managed to hatch and rear at least one chick. This activity was the one which the teachers found hardest to stand back from so as to avoid giving the children any input. The development inside the egg was a golden teaching opportunity which they were reluctant to miss. (An initial problem of locating incubators which worked and could be borrowed, and suppliers of fertile eggs who would be prepared to accept the chicks back once they had hatched, was overcome after diligent searching.)

Children's own height and weight

■

These measurements were to be used as a starting point for discussion based upon the children's experience, since the time span of the classroom work was insufficient for any observable growth to occur. These discussions proved fruitful and were not hampered by lack of available comparative measurements. Comparison between individuals was possible, and this also led to profitable discussion.

Elicitation Techniques

Diaries (free writing/drawing)

■

It was suggested that children should make regular observations of the materials, the frequency depending on the rate of change; plant growth might be looked at every day, and stick insects every week. The diaries could be pictorial or written, depending on the age of the children involved, and any entries could be supplemented by teacher annotations if the children's comments needed explaining more fully. The main purposes of these diaries were to focus attention on the activities and to provide an informal record of the children's ideas.

The teachers of younger children, in particular, found that individual diaries were time-consuming since the children's skills in writing and drawing were not highly developed. The children's entries tended to be descriptive and in this respect they often provided valuable evidence of very careful observation, as in the following example from a six year old's stick insect diary. (Figure 2.1)

Fig. 2.1

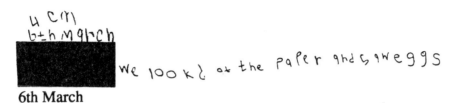

6th March

"We looked at the paper and saw eggs".

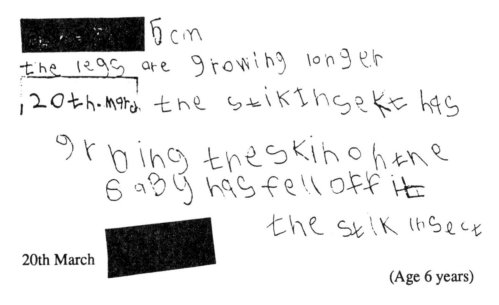

20th March

(Age 6 years)

"The legs are growing longer "

"The stick insect has grown, the skin on the baby has fell off it."

There was also a large number of activities to observe and this proliterated the number of diaries for some children. Nevertheless some of these diaries provided a coherent record of children's thoughts.

Fig. 2.2

> ## Day 5
>
> Now John has suggested that the Seats are the poo and that when they eat they have to get rid of the food that they eat Because they wodd have very bad Stomechach. We have cept the stick-insects for seven days and seven nights. We have put another leave in Wintys bottle but we took it out of the tintys bottle.The Stick-insects live for seven or six months. I thoght that the Stick-insects where two or three months-old I think they like it now. We think one of the dangers for the Stick-insects is that we have not too put them in the sun and keep them in a cool place.

(Age 7 Years)

Day 5

"Now John has suggested that the seeds are the poo and that when they eat they have to get rid of the food that they eat because they would have very bad stomach ache. We have kept the stick insects for seven days and seven nights. We have put another leaf in Winty's bottle but we took it out of Tinty's bottle. The stick insects live for seven or six months. I thought that the stick insects were two or three months old. I think they like it now. We think one of the dangers for the stick insects is that we have not to put them in the sun and keep them in a cool place."

It was suggested that an alternative to individual diaries, particularly for younger children, might be group or class diaries. These could be placed beside the activity so that any child could make an entry (named and dated) as and when they had a comment or observation to offer . These group diaries worked very well and it was found that one child writing or drawing encouraged others to contribute.

Fig. 2.3

Fig. 2.3

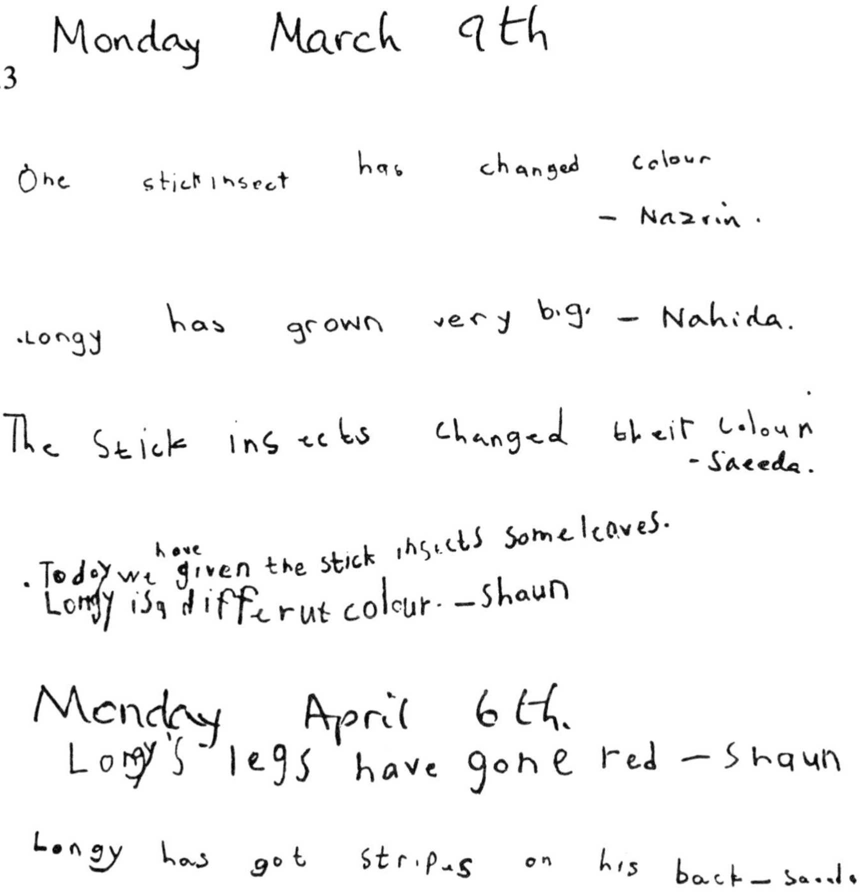

The following is a handwritten diary entry:

Monday March 9th

One stick insect has changed colour
— Nazrin.

.Longy has grown very big. — Nahida.

The Stick insects changed their colour
—Saeeda.

.Today we have given the stick insects some leaves.
Longy is a differut colour. —Shaun

Monday April 6th.
Longy's legs have gone red —Shaun

Longy has got stripes on his back—Saeeda.

"Monday March 9th
One stick insect has changed colour. - Nazrim.
Longy has grown very big. - Nahida
The stick insects changed their colour. - Saeeda
Today we have given the stick insects some leaves.
Longy is a different colour. - Shaun

Monday April 6th
Longy's legs have gone red. - Shaun
Longy has got stripes on his back. - Saeeda"

The status of the diaries, from the teachers' point of view, was in some instances problematic. In the same way that open-ended questioning and an interest in any response might have been considered to be an abrogation of teaching responsibility so too was the acceptance of children being able to write what they chose, as and when they chose to do so. There was a very thin line to divide encouraging children to take an interest in these 'background activities' and allowing them to assume a prominence in order to provide the motivation for children to write or draw in a diary. These informal recording skills had to be developed by the children incidentally; it was not a procedure or format with which many were familiar.

It was gradually realised that the use of the word 'diary' led to an over-emphasis on regular recording, whether there had been any change in the growing materials or not. Reference to a 'diary' also, by association, probably encouraged the recording of factual details without a need being felt to take them any further. Procedures were modified as a result of this experience. The use of the term 'log-book' was substituted in later work.

Structured writing/drawing

Structured writing and drawing was produced particularly in association with the hatching of the hens' eggs. Some classes were directed by their teacher to write about the hatching, and while these accounts were largely factual they came to life when children added details indicating their surprise at the happening, or their expectations of the outcome. One teacher asked the class of children to draw what they thought would be happening inside the egg. These drawings were extremely informative, particularly as the teacher asked children to label their diagrams with explanatory notes and comments following discussion and clarification with her.

Fig. 2.4   Fig. 2.5

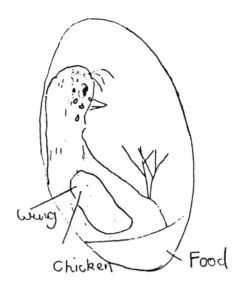

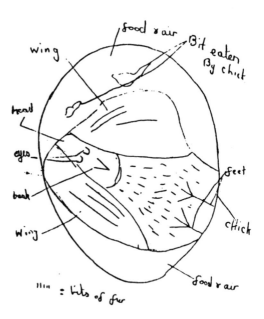

(Age 9-10 years)   (Age 9-10 years)

Individual discussion

■

Some teachers, especially those of younger children, found the diaries to be unproductive and so they kept their own record of children's comments in a notebook. While this procedure was itself time-consuming the teachers concerned found it easier to manage than assisting a whole class of infants with writing, or clarifying drawings.

Class discussion

■

Class discussions were tape-recorded. These tape-recorded discussions were, for many teachers, their first attempt at using a tape-recorder in this way with their class. This novelty, along with what were to some teachers unfamiliar questioning procedures, meant that the dialogue was occasionally rather stilted. Some teachers indicated that their concern to ensure that each child's comment would be identifiable disrupted the flow of the discussion so that it was not as natural as they would have liked.

Classroom Organisation

Two main types of class organisation emerged in connection with this work. Teachers who preferred children to keep individual diaries tended to ask each child to look at all of the activities. Teachers who preferred group diaries tended to allocate a group of children to one activity, though they were not precluded from looking at the rest. The teachers' presentational style might have influenced this choice and on the whole it was felt that dividing the activities amongst groups was more manageable.

Individual Interviews

At the close of the Exploration phase, a sample of children from each participating class was selected, on the basis of ideas that they had expressed, to be interviewed by a member of the research team. The interviews were tape-recorded and later transcribed. The activities about which children were interviewed were selected to provide examples of plant growth in soil and water, and from tubers, as well as animal growth. The activities upon which interviews were based were as follows:

a sprouting potato tuber
germinating mung beans
maize seeds grown in soil
stick insects
hens' eggs and chicks.

Where possible, the interviews were held in the presence of the materials upon which the activities were based so as to reduce the burden on recall and give maximum support to children's attempts to express their ideas. The interviewer had a set of questions around which to base the interview but was not limited to these questions or to a particular order of presentation if further clarification was needed. Interview questions are in Appendix III.

The research team had envisaged the Exploration within the classroom as proceeding in a low-key manner. However, the relative unfamiliarity to many teachers and children of both the unstructured recording and open questioning meant that the activities had received more prominence than had been anticipated.

Estimated times for germination of seeds which were given to the teachers had been produced by growing specimens in the research office. The conditions for growth appeared to be far more favourable in the office than the classroom, with the latent period before visible growth as much as doubled in the classroom.

A vast amount of data from classroom work and individual interviews was collected during the Pilot phase and this formed a valuable bank of information about the views which primary school children hold. The in-depth interviews provided evidence for the existence of a wide range of ideas, some of which had not been anticipated. (Figure 2.5)

Transcript 2.1

(from an interview with a six year-old about stick insects)

Q.   What do you think it is that's making him grow?

R.   *I think it's the ivy.*

Q.   Why do you think that?

R.   *Because it eats the ivy. Every time we eat something we grow a little bit more.*

Q.   Now, you said that every time we eat some food, we grow a little bit. Do you think the same happens to your stick insect every time it eats some food?

R.   *But when he goes to sleep, he grows a little bit as well.*

That growth might occur only in particular circumstances or at particular times had not been incorporated into the interview questions and had not been anticipated. As a result of this and subsequent interviews a question about when growth occurs was added. Secondly, the ease with which teachers handled non-directive teaching experiences in their classroom increased markedly over the five week period. This was mirrored by a greater confidence in their contribution to the project and it enabled them to comment constructively upon the efficacy of particular activities and elicitation techniques within the classroom. These suggestions from teachers were incorporated along with a consideration of practical issues in developing the second exploration phase.

2.2 *EXPLORATION AND ELICITATION TECHNIQUES USED IN THE STUDY*

The structure of this second elicitation period was revised considerably to take into account:

the time of year

a change in the emphasis of the classroom elicitation work

a shorter time span

the fact that this phase was to be followed by the intervention.

The time of year

Autumn is not the time of year which is usually associated with growth. Bearing in mind the importance of a child's experiences in the formation of ideas, it was felt that every effort should be made to avoid growing species of plants which are normally only grown in the Spring or Summer. To this end, it was decided to use mung beans because they can be grown indoors as food at any time of the year. Broad beans were also chosen since they germinated well during the first phase, and are often planted in the Autumn to over-winter. Regrettably, hens' eggs could not be used because of the time of year and the difficulty of finding a supplier who would be prepared to take the chicks back after they had hatched. Instead, eggs laid by Cabbage White butterflies were used, and the caterpillars which hatched were used as the example of animal growth. Teachers were also asked in July 1987 to measure the height and weight of children in the class they would be teaching in September, so that they could be measured again if required in November. This would allow a four-month growing interval so that comparisons could be made using the children's own growth.

A change in the emphasis of the classroom elicitation work

The exploration was intended to be informal but several teachers found this approach to be a departure from their normal way of working and on occasion it became formalised. It was anticipated that this might occur to a larger extent near the start of the school year when teachers were establishing a rapport with their class, even though the technique had become more familiar to them. It was therefore decided to remove the emphasis on the diaries as the main source of children's work and to suggest that children should be given a small number of diagrammatic tasks to encourage their expression of ideas. These labelled diagrams had been extremely productive during the pilot activities in connection with the hens' eggs, so similar questions were posed regarding other aspects of growth. A class 'log-book' was suggested to replace the diaries, and entries were asked for as and when children felt they had something to contribute. Group activities were not suggested as it was felt that this would raise the profile of the activities to an undesirable degree.

A shorter time span

The five-week exploration period had the advantages of enabling material to grow an appreciable amount; chicks were hatched and reared until they were two weeks old, by which age they were growing wing and tail feathers; plant material could germinate and reach a fair size; stick insects grew measurably. On the other hand, it was felt that this period could be rather long to sustain children's interest, particularly that of infants, and the exploration was shortened to two weeks prior to interviewing. This was long enough for the materials to grow noticeably and for children's ideas to be elicited. The number of activities was also reduced in response to the shorter period and teachers' suggestions regarding what was a manageable amount.

Forthcoming intervention

Since the project had an expressed belief in the importance of children's investigative activities in supporting and promoting the development of their ideas it was important that there was potential scope for investigation in at least some of the activities. The broad bean had advantages over maize in that the bean was larger and so could be more easily handled, and the swelling and associated changes which occurred during germination were more easily observable. Animal growth, whatever the organism, was felt to have restricted possibilities for investigation on ethical grounds. It was felt that a checklist based upon the categorization of ideas which emerged during the first exploration might help teachers to form a picture of their classes' ideas in preparation for the intervention.

Teacher guidelines

Teachers were requested to keep the exploratory work as incidental as possible, while establishing the ideas that the children had. The value of 'open' questioning was reinforced, as was the importance of maintaining a non-didactic stance. It was also suggested that the meanings of certain key words, e.g. 'growth', should be probed. Teachers were again provided with written details relating to each activity. These pages are in Appendix IV.

Classroom implementation of the activities

Activities

The activities set up in the classroom were:

> eggs from cabbage white butterflies
> caterpillars
> broad beans grown in soil
> mung beans
> potatoes

Eggs

It was agreed that these eggs should be introduced as 'eggs which caterpillars will come out of', to avoid the potential ambiguity of describing them as butterfly eggs when what would emerge would be caterpillars. The eggs hatched very successfully though because of their size (approximately one millimetre), they had to be viewed through a magnifier. This necessity for magnification does not seem to have been problematic, even with the younger children. In fact, the hatching caused as much interest and excitement as had the hens' eggs.

Caterpillars

The possible dangers of feeding caterpillars on shop-bought cabbage in case it had been sprayed with insecticide were known to the research team who took efforts to obtain organically grown cabbage. Unfortunately, this cabbage had been treated with anti-caterpillar bacteria and many of the caterpillars which were fed on it died. Replacement batches of eggs were obtained from the supplier though these did not seem to thrive. Only six out of twelve classes managed to rear a batch of caterpillars. However, these six classes found it a very profitable activity and they were able to observe feeding followed by rapid growth. The caterpillars were kept until they pupated, over-wintered and hatched out as butterflies.

Broad beans

These germinated and grew very successfully. They were planted in transparent containers so that root growth could be seen even though they were grown in soil.

Mung beans

These again grew successfully and with less rotting than in the first phase since the teachers were familiar with the procedures.

Potatoes

These were almost completely unsuccessful since they failed to sprout.

Elicitation Techniques

Labelled diagrams

Three tasks were set which teachers were asked to introduce in as informal a way as possible so as to avoid the atmosphere of a test. The tasks were to be introduced at the appropriate point in growth or development. The tasks were as follows:

> draw what you think is happening inside the eggs.

- draw a plant in the place you would put it for it to grow very well. Show everything you think the plant would need.
- (drawn when the broad beans were established)

> draw a picture of your caterpillar and what it is doing today. Next to it, draw what you think it will be like tomorrow, and the day after that ... so
- you end up with five pictures.
  (drawn 4 to 5 days after hatching)

These proved to be acceptable and viable classroom techniques, making sufficiently modest demands on teacher time to allow them to discuss the pictures with some of the children and add clarification to the diagrams where necessary. Teachers of children at years one and two found these tasks possible with their classes, though the results were more variable and at times required extensive clarification due to the children's limited recording skills.

Group log-books

The log-books replaced diaries as informal opportunities for recording details felt to be important by the children. They were often large format 'scrapbooks' into which children could paste their entries. They were found to be unobtrusive and helpful as stimuli for individual discussion between the teacher and a child. The content was often limited to factual descriptions, though teachers were becoming more proficient at probing further to obtain elaborations and interpretations.

Individual discussion

Teachers appeared to find this increasingly useful, possibly as their familiarity with open questioning methods increased.

Organisation

The amount of 'Growth' material was felt by teachers to be manageable within the classroom situation and the structured drawings proved very easy to organise. The main concern of teachers appeared to be the lack of time available for one-to-one discussion. It seemed that they had become aware of the potential within each child and wanted to explore it. Several teachers found themselves using break times to talk to children so that they could construct a 'complete picture' of their classes to help them in the intervention.

Individual Interviews

A random, stratified sample of children was selected from each class to be interviewed individually following the exploration. The children were chosen so that there was an equal number of boys and girls from each of the three achievement bands.

The number of activities in this second exploration was small enough to allow the interview to cover all of them. This selection of activities was representative of plant growth in soil and water and from tubers, and animal growth.

The interviewer had a set of questions, similar to those used in the first phase but refined as a result of experiences gained. The interview questions may be found in Appendix V.

The structure of the Exploration proved very successful within the classroom, allowing children to express their ideas in both a structured and an unstructured way. As a result of this phase of work, teachers were able to gain an overview of the ideas emergent in their classes, and to discover similarities between their own and other teachers' children when experiences were exchanged at group meetings.

3. AN INFORMAL LOOK AT CHILDREN'S IDEAS

Children's writing and drawing provided a detailed qualitative overview of their ideas. The individual diaries used in the Pilot, and the group log-books from the Exploration were a useful means of encouraging children to record observations informally. These sources revealed the details children were observing. However, particularly with regard to plant growth, the diaries provided very little evidence for the existence of ideas about the mechanisms of, or necessary conditions for, growth. The introduction of structured drawing tasks during the second exploration was very useful, since the labelled drawings enabled children to express their ideas more fully. The range of ideas articulated was limited to responses to the specific questions asked and these responses mainly provided information about conditions rather than mechanisms. The value of the diagrams was often greatly enhanced by teachers' annotations. This additional labelling not only clarified children's intentions but sometimes extended the ideas expressed so that some indication of mechanisms was revealed.

These diagrams have provided a systematic source of data covering the majority of children in all twelve of the classes involved in 'Growth'. They were easy to incorporate into classroom activities and provided valuable opportunities for teachers to talk to individual children and to build up a picture of each child's understanding. While some cross-fertilisation of ideas might have occurred, children seemed to enjoy the opportunity to draw their own thoughts on paper.

Plant Growth

Children were asked to draw 'a plant' in the place where it would grow best, and to show everything it needed.

The choice of 'plant' to be drawn was interesting. Approximately half of the children chose a broad bean in a transparent container, similar to the one grown in their classrooms. This choice may not be influenced by age, since some children throughout the age range drew a broad bean. However, drawing a different, specific named plant, e.g. a tulip or a rubber plant, was something which only junior children did, which suggests they might be using their previous experience to describe a particular plant in a particular location with which they were familiar.

Fig. 3.1

Fig. 3.2

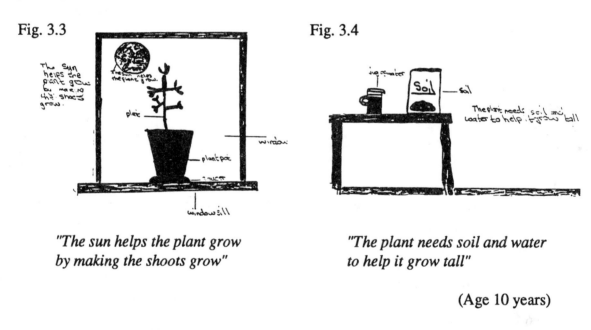

(Age 7 years)

(Age 8 years)

There is a suggestion that the location in which children chose to place the plant varied with age. Infant and lower junior children seemed equally likely to put the plant inside or outside a building while upper junior children nearly all depicted the plant indoors. This difference may indicate an increasing familiarity with house plants as children grow older, and also a wider usage of the term 'plant', including potted plants.

Fig. 3.3

Fig. 3.4

*"The sun helps the plant grow
by making the shoots grow"*

*"The plant needs soil and water
to help it grow tall"*

(Age 10 years)

The range of conditions considered necessary for plants to grow did not seem to be affected by whether the plant was inside or outside, though there appeared to be a tendency for more conditions to be mentioned explicitly when the plant was inside (i.e. labelled conditions rather than simply environmental factors included in the picture). With increasing age, there was evidence of an increasing discrimination in the conditions described. Infant children mentioned only three conditions: water, soil and sun, with few referring to all three. By the lower juniors, some discrimination between the light and heat which are provided by the sun was in evidence, and this was much more marked in the upper juniors where 'light' became a more common response than 'sun'. The number of conditions mentioned by children increased steadily with increasing age though the most commonly mentioned remained water, soil and sun/light/warmth.

Only two children referred to light sources other than the sun.

Fig. 3.4

Fig. 3.5

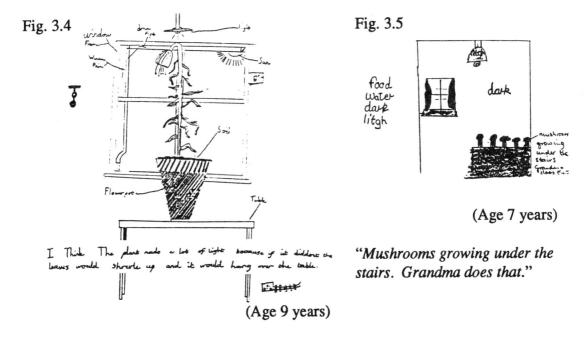

(Age 7 years)

"*Mushrooms growing under the stairs. Grandma does that.*"

(Age 9 years)

"*I think the plant needs a lot of light because
if it didn't the leaves would shrivel up and
it would hang over the table*".

There was very little mention of air or plant food at any age, and no mention at all from the infants. Nearly all mention of plant food was in relation to indoor plants so this condition might be related to the greater experience older children are likely to have had in caring for pot plants. Adequate drainage also tended to be recognised as a requirement of plants in pots only.

Fig. 3.6

(Age 8 years)

Through discussion, teachers of infant children determined that the prevailing view tended to be that the soil was needed to support the plant, rather than for nutrients. This notion might persist into the juniors, though some children seem to be aware of the nutrient value of the soil in providing food for the plant.

Fig. 3.7

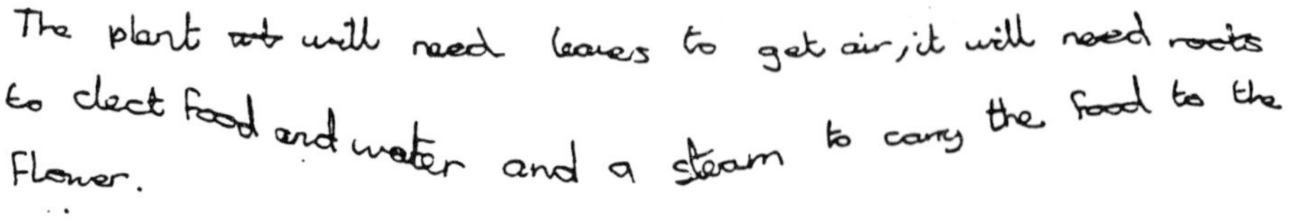

The plant will need leaves to get air, it will need roots to clect food and water and a steam to carry the food to the Flower.

(Age 9 years)

"The plant will need leaves to get air, it will need roots to collect food and water and a stem to carry the food to the flower ."

Growth from onions and root vegetables such as potatoes and carrots, led to some diary entries which appeared to suggest that growth was emanating from a seed situated within the vegetable, or that a plant was growing inside, waiting to push itself out. This idea also emerged during interviews centred on a germinating broad bean.

Fig. 3.8

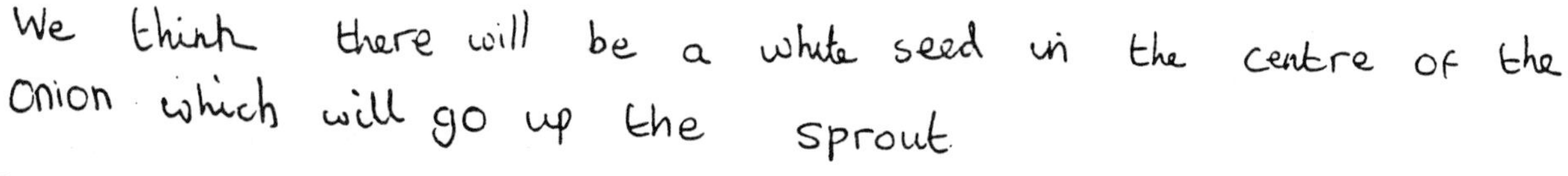

We think there will be a white seed in the centre of the Onion which will go up the sprout

(Age 10 years)

"We think there will be a white seed in the centre of the onion which will go up the sprout ."

Transcript 3.1

(Potato)

Q.   Where do you think the shoots have come from?

R.   *From inside the potato...small little seeds that make stems would be there.....very tiny. You can't see them.*

(Age 10 years)

Transcript 3.2

R.   *The roots will come from the seed that we've planted .*

Q.   What does a seed look like?

R.   *I can't remember.*

Q.   What would you call that? (indicating potato)

R.   *A potato.*

Q.   Is it a seed?

R.   *No.*

Q.   What do potatoes grow from? What do we plant?

R.   *A seed.*

Q.   Why have you planted these in your classroom? (potatoes)

R.   *To see what will happen.*

(Age 10 years)

Also, the dark areas on the tops of carrots, and in the eyes of potatoes were sometimes described as 'soil' from which the new growth was emerging. These notions of soil and seeds being necessary for plant growth may have been reinforced through stories, rhymes and harvest songs with which children are all likely to be familiar. Most plants are also grown from seed so it might be that there have been very few experiences which might lead children to need to seek an alternative idea.

Eggs

Two different types of eggs have been used: hens' eggs in the Pilot phase, and Cabbage White butterfly eggs in the Exploration. Both sets of eggs led to the production of very informative diagrams and writing which are considered here.

Growth inside a fertilized egg is of particular interest because it occurs in a virtually closed system; very little enters or leaves the egg, while part of the contents undergoes a transformation as a result of which the embryo is formed. The nucleus of the yolk (the egg cell) divides and multiplies many times to form the embryo which is nourished by the yolk. The albumen (which also provides water) and the shell are both protective layers, permitting only exchange of gases between the inside of the egg and the atmosphere.

The notion of transformation of material is central to an understanding of growth. In these particular cases, the yolk is being depleted in order to provide energy for cellular growth and development. However, this change cannot be witnessed because of the opacity of the egg shell. This means that any ideas children have about embryo formation within the egg are unlikely to have come from experience of hen's eggs. In some respects this might be regarded as a short-coming in the selection of stimulus material. The more positive view is that, within the context of a highly absorbing and motivating activity, children are required to reveal their general assumptions about growth. Because the transformation of the embryo occurs within a relatively closed system, any changes which are described must be constrained to address mechanisms within that system. The consequences were that children revealed an interesting set of ideas relating to the course and mechanism of animal growth. The range of ideas which emerged are represented schematically in Figure 3.9.

Fig. 3.9

SCHEMATIC REPRESENTATION OF CHILDREN'S IDEAS
ABOUT ANIMAL GROWTH INSIDE AN EGG

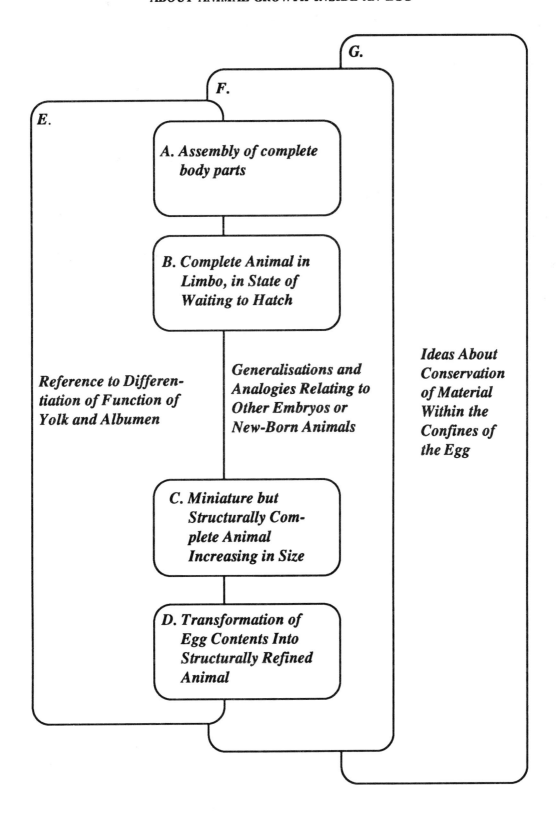

A.   Assembly of Complete Body Parts

This was a fascinating idea, unambiguous when found but infrequently encountered.
The animal inside the egg was described as having been formed as a collection of
component parts which are assembled shortly before hatching.

Fig 3.9

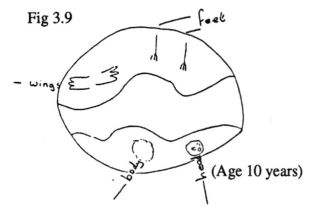

(Age 10 years)

Fig. 3.10

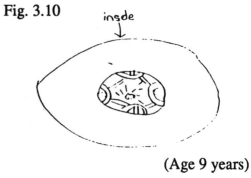

(Age 9 years)

*"I think when the caterpillar grows,
in the egg a leg goes on it."*

B.   Complete Animal in Limbo

The animal inside the egg is completely formed and fully grown from the outset and is waiting to hatch.

Fig. 3.11

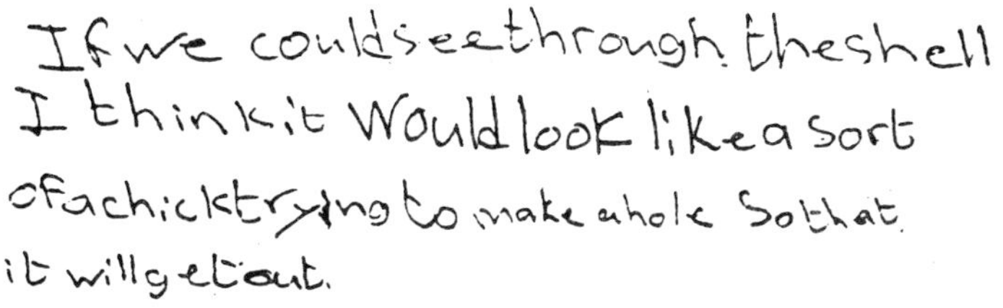

*If we could see through the shell
I think it would look like a sort
of a chick trying to make a hole so that
it will get out.*

(Age 7 years)

"*If we could see through the shell I think it would look like a sort of a
chick trying to make a hole so that it will get out .*"

Fig.3.12

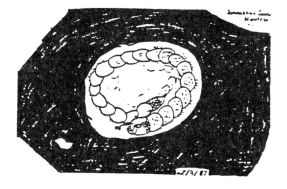

*I think the little caterpillar is scrunched up in that
little egg waiting for his egg to hatch but
while she/he is waiting he/she is planning his life*

(Age 9 years)

"*I think the little caterpillar is scrunched up in that little egg waiting for
his egg to hatch but while she/he is waiting he/she is planning his life* ".

C.   Miniature Animal, Structurally Complete

This was the largest group and within it children described the animal inside the egg
as being completely formed from the outset; it is initially very small and gradually
increases in size. The idea has some parallels with the historical notion of homuncu-
lus, the complete human in miniature form, assumed to be present within the sperm.

Fig. 3.13   Fig. 3.14

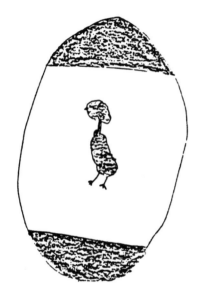

11th March
"If I could see through an egg shell it
it would look like a very little yellow
chick.

(Age 8 years)

11th March
"If I could see through an egg shell it
would look like a very little yellow chick."

(Age 8 years)

"This is inside an egg."

D.   *Transformation of Egg Contents into Structurally Refined Animal*

The idea of the contents of the egg being gradually transformed and refined into the animal structure emerged from some of the older children - it was no doubt influenced by secondary sources. The general description of transformation is perhaps an acceptable approximation to the notion of development of an embryo for children in the primary age range.

Fig. 3.15

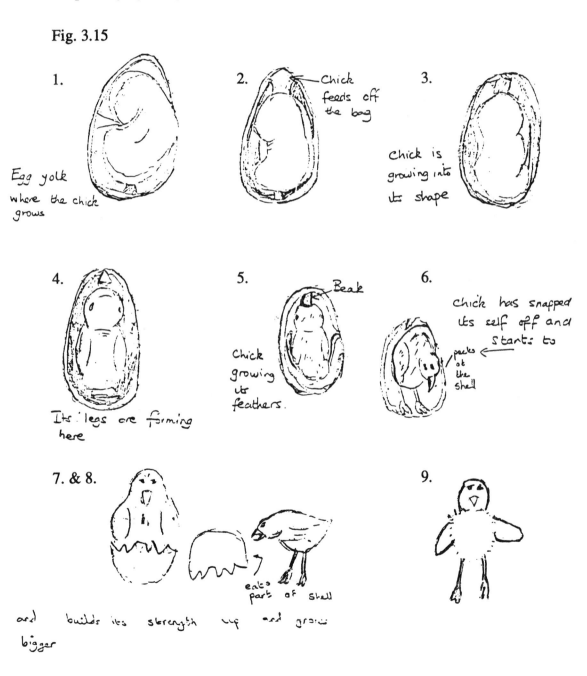

(Some teacher annotations)

Transcript 3.3 indicates the major hazard of secondary sources.

Transcript 3.3

R. *Part of the egg divides up and up and up.*

Q. Which part of the egg David?

R. *Part of the yolk.*

Q. Oh? Not all the yolk?

R. *No it feeds on the yolk*

Q. Oh! How?

R. *From a tube - like a baby in its mother's tummy.*

Q. Then what happens?

R. *Well, it goes on dividing until there are lots - I'd not enough paper.*
  Then it all comes together in a chick shape and it's born.

(Age 10 years)

While some notion of division within the egg has been encountered by this child, even gentle probing reveals the fragility of the particular idea. It seems that, when he lost confidence in his new-found knowledge, this boy resorted to the more familiar explanations of which he was aware, relating probably to human embryology and birth.

E. Reference to Differentiation of Function of Yolk and Albumen

It can be safely assumed that the great majority of children have at some point seen the contents of a hen's egg in its raw form. It is less safe to assume that every child felt driven to construct the conceptual link between a raw egg as seen in the kitchen and a hatching chick in the school's incubator. However, some did attempt to differentiate the function of egg and yolk and this variable adds another dimension to the response categories A to D summarised above.

In Figures 3.16 and 3.17 below, children have depicted structurally complete animals which are using the other contents of the egg as life-support systems. The 'food', 'water' and 'oxygen' sustain the life and growth of the chicks inside the eggs, but no transformaton of the material into body tissue is suggested. Indeed, in Fig. 3.17, the chick is very clearly drawn taking food in through its beak.

Fig. 3.16   Fig 3.17

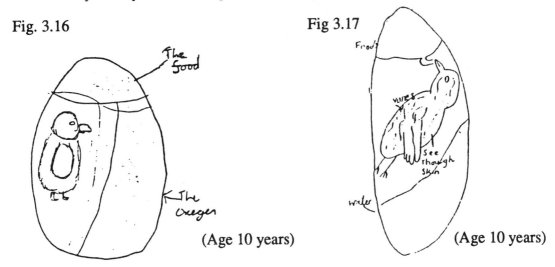

(Age 10 years)   (Age 10 years)

Figures 3.18 and 3.19 represent slight variations on this theme. In 3.18, the suggestion is that the chick 'eats' the yolk, while in 3.19, it is said to feed on the egg-white.

Fig. 3.18   Fig. 3.19

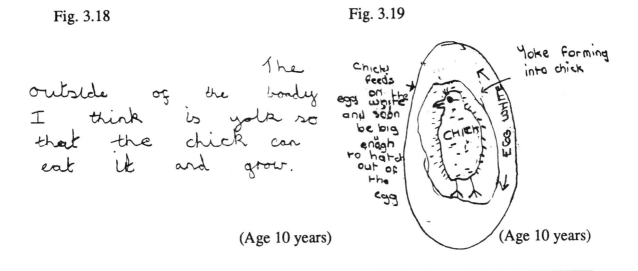

(Age 10 years)   (Age 10 years)

While children might have witnessed the inside of a hen's egg, it was highly unlikely that they had had a similar direct experience with a butterfly's egg. The problem of what the caterpillar would eat within the egg was resolved by some children offering the suggestion that the eggs of the Cabbage White butterfly contained cabbage.

Fig. 3.20

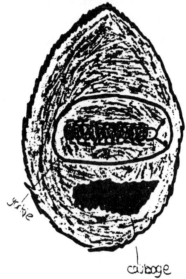

(Age 10 years)

Children who suggested that the chick developed as the result of a transformation of the contents of the egg did, on occasion, attempt to link their knowledge of starting conditions (yolk and white) and finished product (chick). Figure 3.21 shows one such attempt.

Fig. 3.21

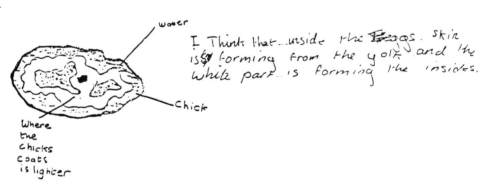

(Age 9 years)

"I think that inside the skin is forming from the yolk and the white part is forming the insides."

It is noticeable in the response illustrated by Fig. 3.21 that the child is holding on to one perceptual attribute common to chick and yolk - colour - and attempting to map these one onto the other.

F. Generalisations and Analogies Relating to Other Embryos

There are some indications as to the experiences children have used to help them explain developments in the relatively unfamiliar fertilized egg. There are three main types of experience which appear to have been brought to bear here: firstly, human foetal development; secondly, the development of tree nesting birds; thirdly, the development of young mammals.

References to movement inside the egg might be generalised from the experience of young babies in the womb, described by mothers or directly felt by children:

"I think that inside the eggs there is growth and they are kicking around inside and they are moving around."

(Age 10 years)

The hen and other birds which have nests on or near the ground hatch much more developed chicks than do birds which nest in trees, In the relative safety of their nest sites above ground, tree nesting birds hatch very dependent young which are initially blind, featherless and needing to be fed. The following idea might stem from experiences with such hatchlings.

"When the eggs hatch the chicken will have no feathers"

(Age 9 years)

One boy appeared to use knowledge of the structure of hens' eggs and the function of the egg-tooth in connection with the caterpillar.

Fig. 3.22

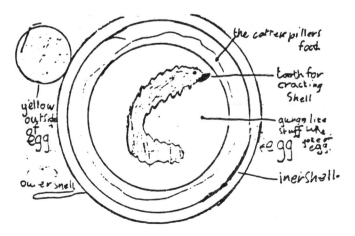

(Age 10 years)

Young mammals, for example, dogs and cats, are born covered in fur but blind. One girl has suggested that :

> *"There will be a body inside of a chicken and it will have feather and no eye site"*

Similarly, with the caterpillar,

Fig. 3.23

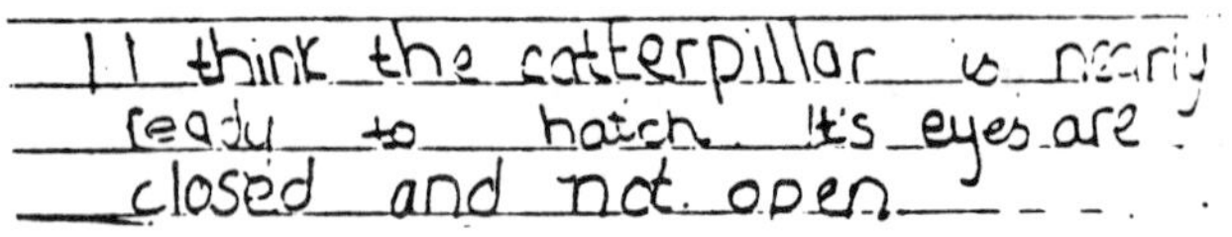

> *I think the catterpillar is nearly
> ready to hatch. It's eyes are
> closed and not open*

(Age 10 years)

> *"I think the caterpillar is nearly ready to hatch. Its eyes are closed and not open."*

The inclusion of such detail makes it seem likely that the children have drawn analogies based on their knowledge of associated areas such as mammalian development.

Some children demonstrated a technical knowledge whch must have been drawn from books or conversations with knowledgeable informants.

Fig. 3.24

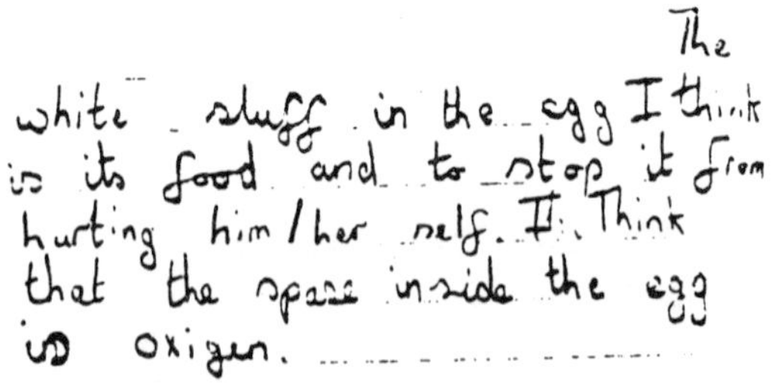

> The
> white stuff in the egg I think
> is its food and to stop it from
> hurting him/her self. I Think
> that the space inside the egg
> is oxigen.

(Age 10 years)

> *"The white stuff in the egg I think is its food and to stop it from hurting him/herself. I think that the space inside the egg is oxygen."*

Some of the children who had an idea of the animal inside the egg increasing in size extended this idea to explain how it was that the shell eventually cracked.

Fig. 3.25

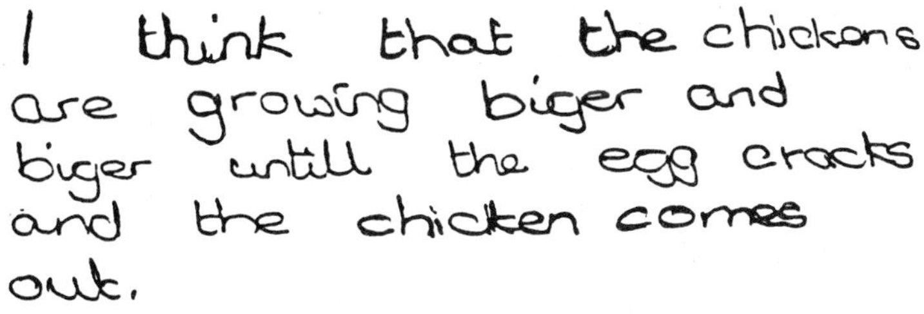

I think that the chickens are growing biger and biger untill the egg cracks and the chicken comes out.

(Age 9 years)

"*I think that the chickens are growing bigger and bigger until the egg cracks and the chicken comes out.*"

Such ideas could have formed valuable starting points for group or class discussion.

G. Conservation of Materials Within the Egg

At a very simple level, growth might be seen by children as simply an *increase* in various dimensions of an organism - height, length, volume, mass. Another critical attribute involved in understanding growth is the process of reoganisation and transformation of material. In an open system, such transformations are accompanied and facilitated by the incorporation of external material. It is fairly safe to assume that young children regard egg shells as impermeable containers (being unaware of the gaseous exchange which occurs). Consequently, questioning children about growth inside eggs offers the opportunity for some insights into their ideas about changes in what may be regarded as a closed system. In the mathematical transformations which Piaget and his colleagues studied and reported (of number, mass, volume, etc.) the changes were *reversible*. It was of interest to the Genevan school to note whether children conserved, e.g. volume, as liquid was poured from one shape of container to another. The changes involved in the processes of growth are *irreversible* but it is of interest to note whether children have any ideas about the conservation of material within an apparently closed system within the eggshell. The following example is provided by a child who has an idea of a miniature but structurally complete caterpillar feeding on an independent support system.

Transcript 3.4

Q.   What do you think happens inside the egg?

R.   *I think the caterpillar eats - you know, when the tadpoles have little jelly beans in their eggs. I think the caterpillars have little jelly beans in their egg and I think they eat it all while they're inside.*

Q.   So, what is in the egg right at the beginning?

R.   *It's some little jelly sort of stuff so when they eat it and when they crack out they could eat the egg after.*

Q.   Right! Now, if we weighed that egg right at the beginning and we weighed it just before the caterpillar came out and we compared the two, what do you think we would find?

R.   *That other one a bit heavier which was before it was ready to come out.*

Q.   A bit heavier - why would it be a bit heavier?

R.   *Because I think the caterpillar might have ate the food.*

Q.   Might have eaten the .... ?

R.   *The jelly bean and it could have gone a bit heavier.*

Q.   So where would the extra weight of the egg come from?

R.   *The caterpillar.*

Q.   From the caterpillar .... ?

R.   *The caterpillar inside of the egg.*

Q.   And it would be heavier because .... why?

R.   *Because he ate plenty of the jelly.*

(Age 10 years)

The caterpillar is eating, growing and getting heavier so the egg will be lighter at the beginning than it will be just before the caterpillar hatches. In this chain of psycho-logic we see the same absence of conservation in an irreversible transformation as has been demonstrated in reversible mathematical transformations. In science, we cannot pour the caterpillar back into the egg!

Assumptions about the overall mass of the egg increasing during the period before hatching were fairly common. The following transcript is a record of an interview with a boy who interpreted growth as stretching. Asked to predict what would be noticed if the egg were weighed at the beginning and towards the end of the incuba-tion period, the dialogue ran as follows:

Transcript 3.5

R.   *It will be nearly exactly the same, just a teeny bit heavier, 'cos the caterpillar, while it's been growing, has been stretching a bit.*

Q.   Where did the extra material come from, to make it heavier?

R.   *It had just stretched, like elastic. It just stretches a bit.*

(Age 10 years)

Another boy made it clear that the overall dimensions of the egg remained constant, despite the increase in mass:

Transcript 3.6

R.   *I think the egg will have stayed the same size but after a bit, the cater-pillar would have grown bigger and therefore it would have been a bit heavier.*

Q.   Where would the material have come from that makes the egg weigh more?

R.   *I think there is some sort of substance in the egg that helps the cater-pillar grow, something that the caterpillar can eat.*

If growth is regarded as a process of creating extra volume, or mass, whether the system within which growth occurs is 'open' or 'closed' is of little consequence. The boundary is not seen as a constraint by these children.

Growth of Caterpillars

Children were asked to draw a caterpillar as it appeared currently and as they thought it would appear on each day for the following four days. There seemed to be little appreciation of time scale on the part of infant children, with caterpillars miraculously turning into butterflies between days four and five. However, it was revealing to note this awareness of metamorphosis in children of infant age.

Fig. 3.26

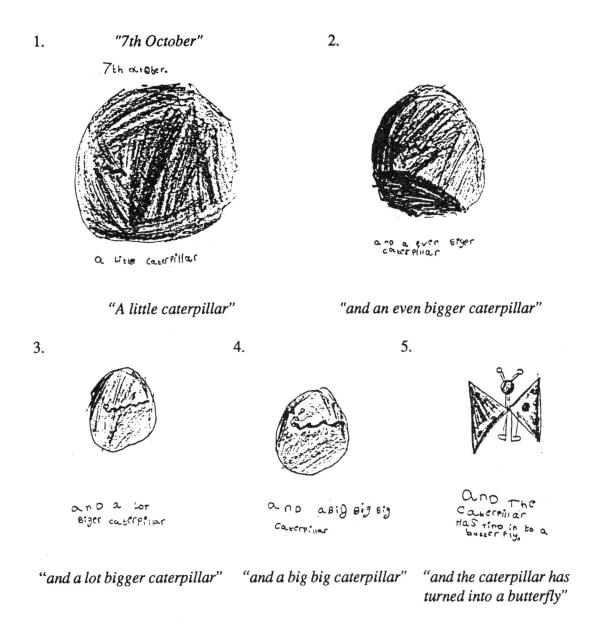

1. *"7th October"*   2.

7th october.

a litte caterpillar

"A little caterpillar"

ano a even biger
caterpiiiar

"and an even bigger caterpillar"

3.   4.   5.

ano a lot
biger caterpiiiar

ano a Big Big Big
Caterpiiiar

Ano The
Caterpiiiar
Has Tino in to a
butterfiy.

"and a lot bigger caterpillar"   *"and a big big caterpillar"*   *"and the caterpillar has
turned into a butterfly"*

One child of lower junior age seemed to be unaware that there might be any further
development and thought that the caterpillar would be dead within five days.

No apparent cause was attributed to growth or to the change of form from caterpillar
to butterfly by most infant children; caterpillars got bigger and bigger but for no
obvious reason. This type of response was found, though less frequently, at every age
up to fourth year juniors. The notion of spontaneous growth may be associated with
the failure of most children to mention or depict droppings.

Children of lower junior age showed some evidence of factual knowledge, with predictions of caterpillars shedding skins. However, much of the growth still seemed to be regarded as spontaneous, unlinked with food intake.

A number of children did relate the intake of food to the increase in size of the caterpillars.

Fig. 3.27

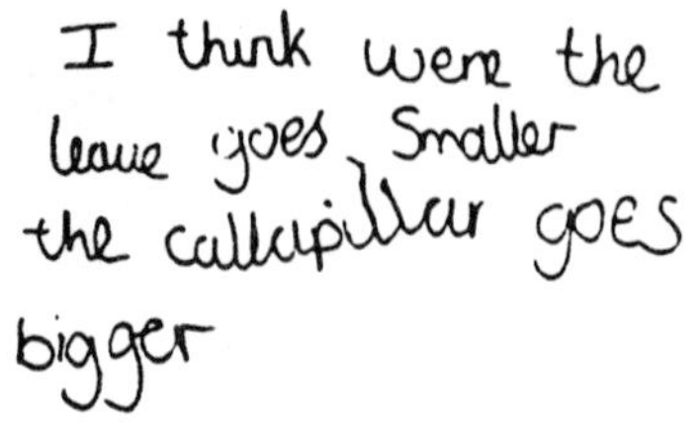

I think were the leave goes Smaller the callupillar goes bigger

(Age 10 years)

"I think where the leaf goes smaller the caterpillar goes bigger ."

It was not uncommon to encounter the idea that the food *intake* was itself the causal factor in growth; that the caterpillar's body was expanding to hold the cabbage. There is no evidence that the food is thought to be transformed at all, or incorporated into the structure of the caterpillar. There is though, the idea that the colour of the caterpillar is changed due to eating the green cabbage.

Fig. 3.28

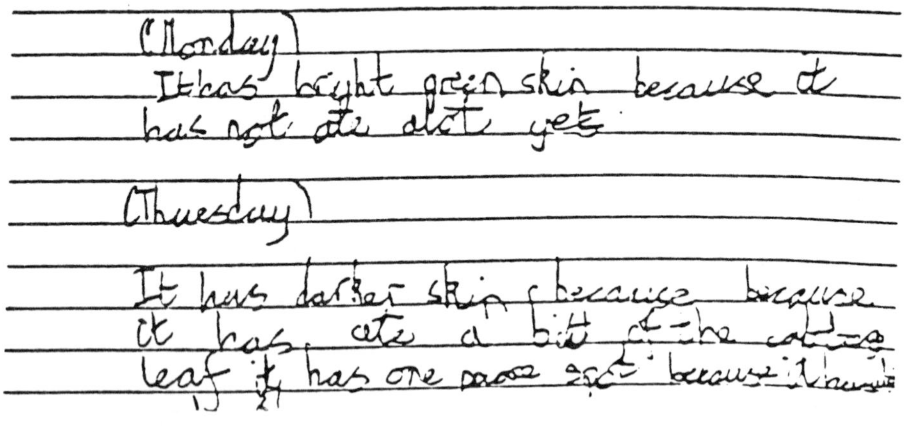

*Monday
It has bright green skin because it has not ate alot yet.

Thuesday

It has darker skin because because it has ate a bit of the cabbage leaf it has one more spot because it has*

*"Monday
It has bright green skin because it has not ate a lot yet."*

*"Tuesday
It has darker skin because it has ate a bit of the cabbage leaf it has one more spot because it has ate"*

(Age 10 years)

The production of droppings was rarely explicitly mentioned, though they were included in the drawings of by some upper junior children and it is only possible to speculate about whether they were connected with food intake and digestion. If this notion of food filling up and stretching the caterpillar is widespread then the likelihood might be that the droppings have been incidentally observed and not connected with the growth process. This could be consistent with the fact that there is only one example of the volume of droppings bearing any relation to the size of the caterpillar, or the amount of food eaten.

Fig. 3.29

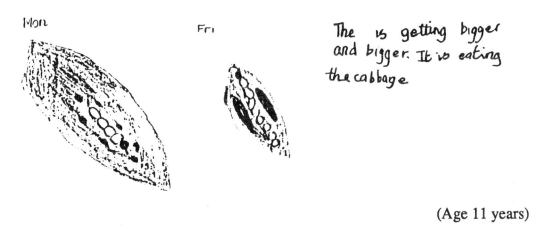

(Age 11 years)

"The (caterpillar) is getting bigger and bigger. It is eating the cabbage."

Further questioning might reveal the existence of a more elaborate notion linking food intake with growth and ingestion, though on the basis of these diagrams any understanding of the growth process seems to be rudimentary. However, the fact that some children of upper junior age are able to make the necessary observations suggests that there might be potential for developing the ideas of incorporation and transformation of food.

4. RESPONSES TO INDIVIDUAL INTERVIEWS

The teachers and children involved in the project generated a tremendous range, volume and quality of data during the course of their classroom activities. These products and activities have particular validity in providing instances and impressions of successes and difficulties encountered in managing pupil-centred learning in the classroom. However, from a research standpoint, where issues such as the reliability and generalisability of the information collected have to be considered, a more controlled form of data collection was also deemed necessary.

Individual interviews with a stratified sample of children held several advantages. Foremost, they permitted the opportunity to explore children's ideas to the point where ambiguity about what children were trying to express was reduced to a minimum. Equally important, by balancing the sample by sex, age and achievement band, generalisations should be possible about the frequency with which certain ideas prevailed. As well as enabling the quality of children's ideas to be discovered, interviews conducted with a random sample introduced the possibility of quantification and statistical treatment.

The logistical demands of large-scale interviewing is the price to be paid for this research rigour, and a compromise was necessary concerning sample size between what would be ideal and what could be collected realistically. It was hoped to collect interview data from twenty children in each of the age groups, infant (5 - 7 years), lower juniors (7 - 9 years) and upper juniors (9-11 years). Sometimes it was possible slightly to exceed these targets; on other occasions there was a shortfall. This must simply be accepted as the reality of working closely with teachers and children, when absences and illnesses occur, when the duration of interviews cannot easily be controlled, and where, on occasions, the plant or animal material which is the focus of interest cannot withstand the rigours of research and itself expires.

The pre- and post-intervention design was also vulnerable to a further erosion of the sample size with the passage of time. This makes comparisons of frequencies of response of *groups* problematic, on occasions. The recording of changes within *individuals* is another, equally valid method of analysing the interview data. Where possible, both methods were used and are reported.

Germination and Growth of Broad Bean in Soil

With the plant material which had been grown providing the focal point for discussion (a broad bean, usually in the range 5 - 15 cm tall) children were questioned to establish their understanding of the nature of the material process of growth, particularly their ideas about the redistribution or transformation of materials. Children were generally very proud of the plants which were the products of their attention, and tended to be very willing to describe their activities.

Sources of New Plant Material in the Broad Bean

The initiating question was, 'Where do you think the leaves have come from?', but questioning pursued responses in order to clarify any emerging notions. Categories of response are summarised in Table 4.1.

Table 4.1   **Broad Bean in Soil: Sources of the New Plant Material; Percentages by Age Group[1]**

	Infant n = 22	Lower Juniors n = 22	Upper Juniors n = 17
From the bean	23 (5)	18 (4)	12 (2)
From *inside* the bean	27 (6)	59 (13)	50 (10)
The stem from the bean, the leaves from the stem/shoots	9 (2)	14 (3)	24 (4)
From under the ground	9 (2)	-	-
Reference to Materials Outside the Bean being Incorporated			
Reference to soil/minerals/compost, etc.	-	-	6 (1)
Reference to water/moisture, etc.	-	-	6 (1)
Reference to air/gases, etc.	-	-	6 (1)
Other	9 (2)	-	-
Don't know	23 (5)	5 (1)	-
No response	5 (1)	5 (1)	-

[1] Percentages are of children in each age group whose responses have been categorised as within the definition in the left-hand column; raw numbers responding are in brackets.

By far the most common response was that the plant material had emerged from the seed. Eighteen per cent of children overall did not elaborate beyond the assertion that the leaves, stems and/or roots came 'from the bean'. The responses of a further 48% of children were less ambiguous, clearly indicating that the leaves, etc. had come from inside the bean. The material mechanism of growth is suggested to be an unfolding, or rearrangement of the material from within the seed.

Q.   Where do you think the leaves have come from?

R.   *Out of the bean - they were inside the broad bean. We didn't see them when they were inside. They were curled inside.*

(Age 11 years)

This type of response was given by just over a quarter of the infants, and about three-fifths of the juniors in the sample.

A more detailed elaboration of the 'unfolding' type of response occurred when a line of questioning pursued an initial assertion that the leaves came from the stem, and the stem from the bean. This kind of response was produced more frequently by the upper juniors (24%) than by infants (9%) or lower juniors (14%).

R.   *They've come from inside the shoot and it was inside the bean..*

(Age 8 years)

The impression is gained that very few children think of plant growth as a process of incorporation of material from outside the plant. Only amongst the older juniors was any reference made to materials outside the bean being incorporated to form the leaves and stem. This was a reference to each of soil/minerals, water and air made by one girl.

Q.   Where do you think the leaves have come from?

R.   *From the soil. From water. From the air outside. That's it.*

(Age 11 years)

The vast majority of children appear to have little idea of the process of plant growth in which materials are incorporated from the external environment of the plant to make new material. The commonly held idea is that plant material comes from the bean or seed. Fifty-nine per cent of responses from infants were of this nature, while 91% of lower juniors and 95% of upper juniors responded in this way. For about two-thirds of junior children, this idea is expressed as more than a location, or direction from which growth occurred. It is explicitly an unfolding. There is reason to suspect that for many children in the primary age range, 'growing' implies the creation of new matter in the form of plant material. To some extent, the 'unfolding' idea is more plausible at the germination stage than it is as a description of mature plant growth. Inevitably, children will have more focused experience of germination, especially within classrooms, than of mature growth of large plants. There is clearly a case for directing children's attention to the growth of plants which increase their mass dramatically - though this is by no means a guarantee that ideas of growth as the generation of matter will not prevail.

Mechanism of Germination and Growth of the Broad Bean

Children's ideas about the mechanism of germination and growth of the bean emerged in response to the question, "What do you think is happening inside the bean (seed)?".

Table 4.2   **Broad Bean in Soil: The Mechanism of Germination and Growth; Percentages by Age Group**

	Infant n = 15	Lower Juniors n = 16	Upper Juniors n = 18
Reforming/reorganisation of materials[1]	-	-	11 (2)
Enlargement; increase in mass/volume/ size	40 (6)	13 (2)	28 (5)
Growth/growing	20 (3)	25 (4)	11 (2)
Water enlarges/softens/swells the bean, is taken in/enters	27 (4)	50 (8)	39 (7)
Roots/shoots push or exert force or are pushed	-	25 (4)	28 (5)
Straightening, uncurling	7 (1)	19 (3)	11 (2)
Seed within a seed	7 (1)	13 (2)	6 (1)
Increase in 'strength' of plant	7 (1)	13 (2)	6 (1)
Other mechanisms	-	-	22 (4)

[1] Some children offered more than one category of response.

It has to be acknowledged that the description of how growth occurs might well be found a challenge by many adults, and perhaps unsurprisingly, few children were able to posit a mechanism. Most responses referred to a causal relationship initiated or sustained by moisture. This type of explanation was more commonly expressed by junior children, coming from 27% of infants, 50% lower juniors and 33% of upper juniors. In tending the seeds and young plants, the provision of water would have been children's major involvement. (The beans themselves swell to perhaps twice their starting volume in a moist environment.) One-fifth of children referred to an enlargement of some kind taking place. The idea of incorporation of material from outside the plant seems to be acceptable in the context of water being involved in the initial stages of germination of the seed. During the individual interviews, only two children referred to material other than water "going in" the bean.

> Q. What happens inside the bean?

> R. *They crack open and the water goes in and a few bits of soil and they make the shoot come out.*

> (Age 8 years)

Whether or not the soil has any function in relation to the bean is not clear in this instance. The second response referring to material other than water was the following:

> R. *The shoots made a hole; the oxygen and air have started to go inside the seed.*

> (Age 11 years)

Once again, the mechanism itself is not elaborated, but it seems that 'oxygen and air' have some part to play.

Some responses approached a notion of energy in the system. Most explicit, but only coming from children of junior age (9 children, 26% of the 34 interviewed) was the idea of the roots or shoots pushing or exerting force. These responses are not indicating the source of the energy, only that it is there.

Ten per cent of the sample referred to 'straightening' or 'uncurling' taking place, which might be understood to be an oblique reference to a source of energy, as in a coiled spring. Four children (8%) referred to the bean as gaining in 'strength'.

The idea of a seed within a seed was one which had been heard during the Pilot exercise in relation to onions, carrots and potatoes. It was perhaps more surprising to find it used in connection with the broad bean, but there is no doubting the meaning which these children intended to convey.

> R.   *There's a little bean inside the bean which makes a stem and grows the leaves, and the roots come from that, as well. There is a big fat layer on top.* (Assumed to be a reference to the 'outer, visible' bean.)

> (Age 11 years)

Only two children, both in juniors, referred to a re-organisation of the material within the bean.

> R.   *For a few days the ingredients mix together and stick together, then come out."*

> (Age 10 years)

Conditions Necessary for Growth of the Broad Bean

It was of interest to elicit ideas about the *conditions* for growth as well as the *mechanism*. 'What do you think the plant needs to help it grow?' and 'What do you think makes it grow and how?' were questions which elicited comments about either aspect. Table 4.3 summarises references to variables or conditions for the growth of the broad bean in soil identified by the three age groups.

Table 4.3 **Suggested Conditions Necessary for Growth of Broad Bean: Percentages by Age Group**

	Infant n = 20	Lower Juniors n = 24	Upper Juniors n = 18
Air[1]	-	-	22 (4)
Oxygen	-	-	11 (2)
Carbon dioxide	-	-	-
Sun	25 (5)	21 (5)	22 (4)
Light	5 (1)	8 (2)	22 (4)
Warmth/heat	5 (1)	13 (3)	39 (7)
Water/moisture/damp	85 (17)	100 (24)	83 (15)
Soikl/compost/sand	30 (6)	29 (7)	56 (10)
Plant food/minerals/fertiliser	5 (1)	4 (1)	11 (2)
Soil cover	-	-	6 (1)
Creatures (in or above soil)	-	4 (1)	6 (1)
Darkness	-	8 (2)	11 (2)
Cool	-	4 (1)	6 (1)
The bean/roots/leaves (tautology)	20 (4)	4 (1)	6 (1)

[1] Some children suggested more than one condition

Only from the upper juniors was there any reference to gases of any kind being necessary for plant growth; such knowledge would only have been acquired from transmitted sources (books, family discussion, films and television or direct instruction). The four responses emanated from two of the six schools involved in the 'Growth' topic; the two references to 'oxygen' were from one school.

R. *It needs a bit of air, a few holes for the air to get to it.*

(Age 9 years)

R. *Oxygen has given the plant the air to come up and warmth has given it the warmth to expand and get bigger.*

(Age 11 years)

R. *A wet and damp place. Oxygen and air, soil and water.*

(Age 11 years)

'Oxygen' and 'air' were offered as conditions, but without any description, explicit or implicit, about their function.

The sun was mentioned as a condition by about a quarter of children in each age group. Mention of 'light' might be thought of as a more sophisticated differentiation of the properties of the sun; its use increased with age, as did reference to warmth or heat.

Water, moisture or dampness as a pre-requisite for plant growth was mentioned by 90% of children, overall. Watering the plants would have been children's main involvement; they were also growing mung beans as a separate activity, so the association with plant growth would be expected to have been noticed.
The acknowledgement of the need for soil was forthcoming from about one-third of infants and lower juniors, and over half of the upper juniors.

The number of conditions which children were able to relate to the growth requirements of broad beans rose significantly with age, as Table 4.4 shows.

Table 4.4   Broad Bean in Soil: Number of Conditions Identified as Helpful for Growth; Percentages by Age Group

Number of Conditions Identified	Infant n = 20	Lower Juniors n = 24	Upper Juniors n = 18	All n = 62
None	10 (2)	-	-	3 (2)
One	40 (8)	25 (6)	-	23 (14)
Two	40 (8)	58 (14)	17 (3)	40 (25)
Three	10 (2)	13 (3)	72 (13)	29 (18)
Four	-	4 (1)	11 (2)	5 (3)
Totals	100(20)	100(24)	100(18)	100(62)
Mean No. of Conditions Identified	1.5	1.9	2.8	2.1

The mean number of conditions identified by the three age groups may be presumed to reflect developmental differences in information processing capacity. These relative differences need not be thought of as absolute values, implying a ceiling of expectation, but are a reminder of the differences which can be expected within the age range interviewed.

Ideas about When Growth Occurs in the Broad Bean

It is fairly widely accepted that in young children thinking is often found to be perceptually dominated. Children 'know' what they can perceive. Unfortunately, perhaps, some phenomena or aspects of the world which are important to understand are imperceptible by nature. The process of plant and animal growth is one such imperceptible change. In these circumstances, it does not seem to be the case that children suspend judgement pending the accessibility of the complex chain of reasoning and description formulated by scientists. When perceptible evidence exists, children might well be dominated by it; when it does not, they are frequently willing to give explanations in terms of a causal link between two states. During the pilot phase, some interesting ideas about when growth occurred had emerged, so it was decided to include questions about the time of occurrence and limits of growth. In response to the question, 'When do you think the plant grows?', responses as categorised in Table 4.5. emerged.

Table 4.5   **Broad Beans in Soil: Ideas about When Growth Occurs; Percentages by Age Group**

	Infant n = 21	Lower Juniors n = 23	Upper Juniors n = 182
Continuously, little by little, day and night	24 (5)	35 (8)	50 (9)
During the day/morning	14 (3)	4 (1)	28 (5)
At night	14 (3)	22 (5)	28 (5)
Related to seasons/calendar	14 (3)	22 (5)	-
When external conditions are suitable (e.g. food/water available)	19 (4)	22 (5)	-
In pupils' absence	5 (1)	4 (1)	-
Other	5 (1)	-	6 (1)
Don't know	5 (1)	9 (2)	-
Totals	100(21)	100(23)	100(18)

The idea of continuous growth, is perhaps is the most accurate description that could be hoped for from the age group. This idea steadily increases in frequency across the three age groups, from about a quarter of infants to a third of lower juniors, and a half of the upper juniors. The idea of things growing at night or in pupils' absence seems to emerge from a line of reasoning which runs, 'It's grown. I didn't see it growing. It must have grown when I wasn't here, or wasn't looking'. The idea of plants or animals growing at night was also encountered in children's descriptions of their own growth. Over a quarter of upper juniors suggested that the broad bean grew during the night. This notion is problematic in relation to the progression of learning; it is not untrue, but it obscures a consideration of the crucial contribution of light (and perhaps warmth).

Ideas About the Limits of Growth of the Broad Bean

The lack of order in the world as perceived by infants was revealed during classroom activities when some children questioned what range of plants might grow from the single seed type which was planted. To some children, the possibilities were limitless and this is a most important finding in considering progression in this area of the curriculum. The idea of species variability is an important one to establish; children can readily perceive individual differences within their own class, for example. But there are other aspects of growth which call for a recognition of limits and ranges of variability and the understanding of a pre-determined course of development programmed within the seed. (Issues of genetic and environmental variability would not be expected to be considered at this point.) Table 4.6 summarises children's ideas about the limits of growth of the Broad Bean.

Table 4.6   **Broad Bean in Soil: Expectations of Limits of Growth; Percentages by Age Group**

	Infant n = 20	Lower Juniors n = 21	Upper Juniors n = 18
No acknowledgement of limit to continued growth	40 (8)	33 (7)	11 (2)
Growth anticipated to stop eventually; life-span and size of plant indeterminate	20 (4)	10 (2)	-
Plant anticipated to stop growing and/ or die at pre-determined size	20 (4)	33 (7)	11 (2)
Plant anticipated to stop growing and/ or die after pre-determined duration	5 (1)	5 (1)	11 (2)
Stops growing and/or dies after pre-determined size and duration	-	-	50 (9)
Stops growing at a stage	-	14 (3)	17 (3)
Other	5 (1)	-	-
Don't know	5 (1)	5 (1)	-
No response	5 (1)	-	-
Totals	100(20)	100(20)	100(18)

While about half of the infant group indicated no acknowledgement of a limit to growth, this was reduced to a third of the lower junior group, and only eleven per cent of the upper juniors. Half of the upper juniors suggested that the plant would stop growing at a pre-determined size and duration of growth. It would be of great interest to know how this understanding emerges, especially the part played by formal education and experience of plant growth in the family garden.

Growth of Mung Beans

Mung beans were soaked in water, drained, and left in a dark warm environment to sprout. It was hoped that the provision of plant material growing in different circum-stances - in this instance, the visible splitting of the seed case and emergence of roots and shoots - might provide the discussion material for a clear understanding of what children thought might be happening in a way which would complement the ideas which emerged about the growth of the broad beans.

Sources of New Plant Material in the Mung Bean

Table 4.7 summarises responses to questions about the source of new plant material in the mung bean. In fact, the incidence of responses suggesting that the seed alone is the source of all new growth is slightly higher than for the broad bean. (See Table 4.1)

Table 4.7 **Mung Bean: Sources of the New Plant Material; Percentages by Age Group.**

	Infant n = 21	Lower Juniors n = 17	Upper Juniors n = 18
Reference to materials inside the bean			
From the bean	14 (3)	29 (5)	11 (2)
From *inside* the bean	52 (11)	65 (11)	78 (14)
The stem from the bean, the leaves from the stem/shoots	5 (1)	6 (1)	11 (2)
Reference to materials outside the bean being incorporated			
Reference to soil/minerals/compost, etc.	-	-	-
Reference to water/moisture, etc.	5 (1)	-	6 (1)
Other	5 (1)	-	-
Don't know	19 (4)	-	-
No Response	5 (1)	-	-

Mechanism of Germination and Growth of the Mung bean

The mechanism of growth of the mung bean was probed with the question 'What do you think is happening within the bean (seed)?'. Responses are summarised in Table 4.8. The effect of water was most frequently mentioned, but less so than had been the case with the broad bean (24% overall for mung beans compared with 39% for broad beans, see Table 4.2, page 45). The age trend, an increasing reference to water with age, was steeper in relation to the mung bean. It is also emphasised that only a minority of responses clearly indicated that water was actually *taken into the seed*. This point is developed further in the next section, when conditions perceived as necessary for growth are discussed.

Table 4.8   **Mung Bean in Water: the Mechanism of Germination and Growth; Percentages by Age Group**

	Infant n = 13		Lower Juniors n = 15		Upper Juniors n = 18	
Reforming/re-organisation of materials	-		7	(1)	17	(3)
Enlargement; increase in mass/ volume/size	23	(3)	33	(5)	17	(3)
Growth/growing	23	(3)	27	(4)	28	(5)
Water enlarges/softens/swells the bean, is taken in/enters	15	(2)	20	(3)	44	(8)
Roots/shoots push or exert force or are pushed	-		13	(2)	11	(2)
Straightening, uncurling	15	(2)	13	(2)	17	(3)
Seed within a seed	-		20	(3)	-	
Increase in 'strength' of plant	-		-		6	(1)

Four children, all juniors, referred to a reorganisation of material. Enlargement of some kind was mentioned overall, at a similar level as with the broad bean. The roots or shoots pushing or exerting a force was an idea which occurred with only half the frequency in reference to the mung bean, as compared to responses referring to the broad bean (See Table 4.2).

The idea of a seed within a seed was offered by three children, but not the same three who had made a similar suggestion for the broad bean.

The only material suggested as being incorporated from outside was water.

Conditions Necessary for Growth of the Mung Bean

Table 4.9. summarises children's suggestions as to the conditions necessary for growth of the mung bean. Five children referred to air as being a necessary condition for the growth of the mung bean; one child mentioned air and oxygen. This group of five included the four children who specified air as a condition for growth of the broad bean; the fifth child was from one of the schools whose pupils referred to a gas of some kind (see also Table 4.3., p. 48)

Table 4.9   Suggested Conditions for Growth of Mung Bean;
Percentages by Age Group

	Infant n = 22	Lower Juniors n = 17	Upper Juniors n = 18
Air	-	-	28 (5)
Oxygen	-	-	6 (1)
Carbon Dioxide			
Sun	5 (1)	6 (1)	11 (2)
Light	-	12 (2)	17 (3)
Warmth/heat	-	18 (3)	28 (5)
Water/moisture/damp	73 (16)	100 (17)	100 (18)
Soil/compost/sand			6 (1)
Plant food/minerals/fertiliser			11 (2)
Darkness	9 (2)	18 (3)	28 (5)
Cool			6 (1)
The bean/roots/leaves (tautology)	9 (2)	6 (1)	6 (1)

All the juniors and 73% of the infants recognised water as a necessary condition for the growth of the mung bean, yet when this finding is compared with the frequency of references to water as playing a part in the *mechanism* of growth (Table 4.8, p. 55) an interesting discrepancy emerges. It would appear that while almost all children recognise water as a necessary condition for growth, it is as an external facilitator or catalyst, rather than something which becomes part of the fabric of the bean or part of the process of growth. (Washing the beans was part of the procedure).

Children were able to identify fewer conditions, on average, relating to the growth of the mung bean than the broad bean (Table 4.10). The age trend of increasing ability to nominate necessary conditions with age was once again apparent.

Table 4.10   **Mung Bean: Number of Conditions Identified as Helpful for Growth; Percentages by Age Group**

	Infant n = 22	Lower Juniors n = 19	Upper Juniors n = 18	All n = 59
Number of Conditions Identified				
None	9 (2)	11 (2)	-	7 (4)
One	77 (17)	47 (9)	11 (2)	48 (28)
Two	14 (3)	32 (6)	44 (8)	29 (17)
Three	-	11 (2)	33 (6)	14 (8)
Four	-	-	11 (2)	3 (2)
Mean No. of Conditions Identified.	1.1	1.4	2.4	1.6

Ideas About When Growth Occurs in the Mung Bean

The ideas which were offered concerning when mung bean growth occurs are summarised in Table 4.11. The fact that the beans were kept in a dark place while they were sprouting did not produce a dramatic increase in any of the categories where it might have been expected, for example in the number of children suggesting that growth occurred at night.

Table 4.11   Mung Bean: Ideas about when Growth Occurs;
              Percentages by Age Group

	Infant n = 19	Lower Juniors n = 15	Upper Juniors n = 18
Continuously, little by little, day and night	21 (4)	33 (5)	28 (5)
During the day/morning	11 (2)	7 (1)	-
At night	21 (4)	-	33 (6)
Related to seasons/calendar	5 (1)	7 (1)	6 (1)
When external conditions are suitable (e.g. food/water available)	11 (2)	20 (3)	28 (5)
In child's absence	5 (1)	7 (1)	6 (1)
Other	11 (2)	7 (1)	-
Don't know	16 (3)	20 (3)	-

Ideas About the Limits of Growth of the Mung Bean

Children's expectations of the limits of growth of the mung bean are presented in Table 4.12.

Table 4.12   **Mung Bean: Expectations of Limits of Growth;**
                   Percentages by Age Group

	Infant n = 18	Lower Juniors n = 17	Upper Juniors n = 18	All n = 53
No acknowledgement of limit to continual growth	66 (12)	17 (3)	6 (1)	30 (16)
Growth anticipated to stop eventually; life-span and size of plant indeterminate	16 (3)	35 (6)	6 (1)	19 (10)
Plant anticipated to stop growing and/or die at pre-determined *size*	6 (1)	18 (3)	16 (3)	13 (7)
Plant anticipated to stop growing and/or die at pre-determined *duration*	-	12 (2)	16 (3)	9 (5)
Stops growing and/or dies after pre-determined *size* and *duration*	6 (1)	-	44 (8)	17 (9)
Stops growing at a *stage*	6 (1)	6 (1)	6 (1)	6 (3)
Other	-	6 (1)	-	2 (1)
No Response	-	6 (1)	6 (1)	4 (2)
Totals	100 (18)	100 (17)	100 (18)	100 (53)

Thirty per cent of the sample indicated no acknowledgement of a limit to the growth of the mung bean - about the same frequency as for the broad bean. However, the age effect was much more noticeable with the mung bean, with two-thirds of infants indicating no awareness of the limits to growth. (Forty per cent of infants indicated no acknowledgements of a limit to the growth of broad beans. See Table 4.6, page 52) The unusual growing environment might be a contributory factor, but it is difficult to specify how.

Changes Within the Eggs of the Cabbage White Butterfly

Children were asked about changes inside the egg of the Cabbage White Butterfly, about conditions necessary for growth inside the egg and about the mechanism of growth.

The first question posed in the context of caterpillar eggs was about what children thought happened inside the egg. Responses are summarised in Table 4.13.

Table 4.13   Children's Ideas About What Happens Inside the Cabbage White Butterfly's Eggs; Percentages by Age Group

	Infant n = 18	Lower Juniors n = 24	Upper Juniors n = 18	All n = 60
Reforming, reorganising of materials	-	4 (1)	6 (1)	3 (2)
Enlargement	-	17 (4)	50 (9)	22 (13)
Growing	-	8 (2)	17 (3)	8 (5)
Feeding (taking in solids)	-	-	44 (8)	13 (8)
Drinking (taking in liquids)	-	-	-	-
Change of form	-	-	6 (1)	2 (1)
Change of colour	-	-	6 (1)	2 (1)
Change of postion/orientation	11 (2)	8 (2)	6 (1)	2 (1)
Movement	-	-	6 (1)	2 (1)
Resting/Sleeping	-	-	6 (1)	2 (1)
Gathering strength	-	-	6 (1)	2 (1)
Trying to get out	-	21 (5)	17 (3)	(8)

Infants were able to offer very little comment about what was happening, unseen inside the eggs. Amongst those older children willing and able to speculate, enlargement of the caterpillar was by far the most common response, being offered by half of the upper juniors: additionally, some children used a more specific reference to 'growth'. Forty-four per cent of upper juniors suggested that the caterpillar would be feeding or taking in solids in some way, but no children suggested the incorporation of liquids. Only two children, one lower and one upper junior, indicated that any reforming or reorganising of materials was taking place inside the egg.

The only other suggestions made in any numbers referred to movement and attempts at emerging from the egg. As with the hen's eggs, there were some suggestion of analogies with the human foetal condition:

> *"The little caterpillar is rolled up and he's eating the little bit of egg from the inside and kicking his legs, trying to get out"*

(Age 10 years)

Table 4.14 summarises the number of comments offered concerning what was happening inside the egg. The age trend was extremely steep; every child in the upper junior age range was able to make at least one suggestion.

Table 4.14   Number of Comments on What Happens Inside Cabbage White Butterfly's Eggs; Percentages by Age Group

	Infant n = 18	Lower Juniors n = 24	Upper Juniors n = 18	All n = 60
None	94 (17)	79 (19)	-	60 (36)
One	6 (1)	-	61 (11)	20 (12)
Two	-	8 (2)	17 (3)	8 (5)
Three	-	13 (3)	22 (4)	12 (7)
Mean Number of Comments	0.3	0.5	1.6	0.7

p<0.0001, chi square 44.5, d.f. = 6

Children were also asked 'What do you think the caterpillar needs to make it grow inside the egg?'. Responses are summarised in Table 4.15, where it can be seen that it was only the upper juniors who really engaged with this question. Food was suggested to be a necessary condition by three quarters of upper juniors, 'drink' by about a quarter. Air or oxygen were mentioned by about a quarter of children, while warmth and protection were each mentioned by 17%.

Table 4.15   **Necessary Conditions for Caterpillar Growth Inside the Egg; Percentages by Age Group**

	Infant n = 18	Lower Juniors n = 24	Upper Juniors n = 18	All n = 60
Food	-	8 (2)	78 (14)	27 (16)
Drink	-	-	22 (4)	7 (4)
Warmth	-	-	17 (3)	5 (3)
Air/Oxygen	-	4 (1)	28 (5)	10 (6)
Safety/Protection	-	-	17 (3)	5 (3)
Other	-	8 (2)	28 (5)	12 (7)

The number of conditions mentioned by each age group is summarised in Table 4.16.

Table 4.16   **Number of Conditions Suggested as Necessary for Caterpillar Growth Inside the Egg; Percentages by Age Group**

	Infant n = 18	Lower Juniors n = 24	Upper Juniors n = 18	All n = 60
None	100 (18)	83 (20)	6 (1)	65 (39)
One	-	17 (4)	39 (7)	18 (11)
Two	-	-	33 (6)	10 (6)
Three	-	-	17 (3)	5 (3)
Four	-	-	6 (1)	2 (1)
Mean Number of Conditions:	0	0.7	1.8	0.6

p<0.0001 chi square 45.2, d.f. = 8

Some of the upper juniors offered thoughtful responses including more than one aspect of the embryo's requirements:

> "I think it needs to be kept flat somewhere, not to be rolled about. I think it needs to go on a leaf. It needs to be kept warm, and I think it needs air."

> (Age 10 years)

For the majority of children, envisaging what was happening inside the egg was difficult enough. Even more difficult was the task of describing the mechanism of growth, which was invited by asking, 'How do you think these things help it to grow? What do you think makes the caterpillars grow in eggs?' About a quarter of upper juniors suggested that the caterpillars increased their dimensions in some way, by length, volume or mass. (See Table 4.17).

Table 4.17   Mechanism of Growth Inside Egg of Cabbage White Butterfly; Percentages by Age Group.

	Infant n = 18	Lower Juniors n = 24	Upper Juniors n = 18	All n = 60
The conditions help it to grow; no elaboration	-	-	17 (3)	5 (3)
Conditions help it to increase in size/length/volume/mass	-	-	28 (5)	8 (5)
The caterpillar gains ' strength ' inside the egg	-	-	28 (5)	8 (5)
The caterpillar gains ' health ' inside the egg	-	-	6 (1)	2 (1)
The conditions cause the caterpillar to ' stretch ' inside the egg	-	-	11 (2)	3 (2)
Other mechanisms	-	8 (2)	6 (1)	5 (3)

Just as with Table 4.7 (Page 54) their descriptions of the growth of the mung bean, it was apparent that some children's assumption that new material was being created or spontaneously generated inside the egg was by no means exceptional.

*"The egg's gone a bit heavier because the caterpillar's grown stronger
and bigger. Without the caterpillar in it, the egg's a bit light, because
the caterpillar's eaten a bit from the inside, most of the egg."*

(Age 10 Years)

*"The one that's almost hatched would be heavier because the
caterpillar inside it is bigger."*
"Where would the extra material come from?"
"The egg."

(Age 10 years)

*"When it's just laid it would be lighter because the caterpillar's very,
very small, and when it's nearly hatched out it would be heavier
because it's grown."*

(Age 10 years)

*"I think the egg will have stayed the same size but after a bit, the
caterpillar would have grown bigger and therefore it would have been
a bit heavier ..... I think there's some sort of substance in the egg that
helps the caterpillar grow, something that the caterpillar can eat."*

(Age 10 years)

These explantions indicate that the children offering them are making no assumptions about conservation of matter within the egg. (The gaseous exchange occuring through the egg-shell is negligible in the context of this discussion). It seems unlikely that children will see the need for any mechanism involving transformation or re-organisation of material until the egg is seen as a (relatively) closed system within which new material cannot be generated.

Growth of the Caterpillar of the Cabbage White Butterfly

Children's observations and recordings of the growth of caterpillars provided access to some ideas about animal growth. They were first asked what had happened since they first saw the caterpillar. This was a deliberately open question, used to establish what observations had been made, which features had been found of interest and what descriptions were used to describe the process of growth. Responses are summarised in Table 4.18.

**Table 4.18   Children's Observations About the Growth of Caterpillars;
Percentages by Age Group**

	Infant n = 18	Lower Juniors n = 24	Upper Juniors n = 18	All n = 60
It's 'Grown' (No further elaboration)	-	13 (3)	22 (4)	12 (7)
Enlarged size/length/volume/mass	28 (5)	33 (8)	39 (7)	33 (20)
Changed colour/pattern	17 (3)	17 (4)	39 (7)	23 (14)
Particular parts of body have grown/ changed (e.g. legs, hairs)	-	4 (1)	6 (1)	3 (2)
Increased activity	-	4 (1)	11 (2)	5 (3)
Feeding noted	28 (5)	25 (6)	11 (2)	22 (13)
Production of droppings noted	-	-	17 (3)	5 (3)

An increase in some dimension of the caterpillar was the change which was most frequently remarked upon, be it size, volume or mass. This kind of comment was offered by one third of children overall; twelve percent of juniors simply referred to the fact that the caterpillar had grown without reference to any specifc aspect. The changed appearance of the caterpillar was noted by about a quarter of children, overall. Feeding was noted by 22% overall, with this kind of observation less common from upper juniors - perhaps because they regarded feeding as too obvious to warrant comment. A very small number of juniors, 5% or less, mentioned one or more of three other aspects : changes in particular features of the body, increased activity and the production of droppings. Only a relatively small number of the oldest group (17%) mentioned the droppings. Whatever the reason for this, it was not that the droppings were not noticeable. Some children may have felt embarassment or difficulty in choosing a word.

It is probably fair to comment that substantive observations were fairly scarce, even those referring to what might be regarded as obvious changes. As Table 4.19 shows, there was an overall average of one observation per child.

Table 4.19   Number of Observations Made About the Growth of Caterpillars; Percentages by Age Group

	Infant n = 18	Lower Juniors n = 24	Upper Juniors n = 18	All n = 60
None	67 (12)	50 (12)	33 (6)	50 (30)
One	6 (1)	21 (5)	11 (2)	13 (8)
Two	17 (3)	17 (4)	33 (6)	22 (13)
Three	11 (2)	8 (2)	17 (3)	12 (7)
Four	-	4 (1)	6 (1)	3 (2)
Mean Number of Observations	0.7	1.0	1.5	1.0

$p < 0.5$ (chi square 7.1, d.f. =8)

Only one third of infants offered any substantive observation; this proportion increased to half the lower juniors and two thirds of the upper juniors. The overall average is inflated by a minority of children who offered two, three or four observations, sometimes of a very sensitive quality:

> *"They've gone a bit bit bigger. They've turned pale green. They've got black spots on the green. They like being in the shade. All the little caterpillars are under the leaves."*
>
> (Age 10 years)

The mean number of observations offered increased steadily with age. Comments on the necessary conditions for caterpillar growth were invited by asking, 'Does the caterpillar need anything to help it grow?' A reference to food was by far the most common condition cited, with almost half the sample referring to 'lettuce' or 'cabbage' or some other generic term. (See Table 4.20). This was the only condition mentioned by infants. It is interesting to note that the next most commonly mentioned condition was a need for air or oxygen, in that this reference draws on knowledge rather than observation. Drink, warmth and shade were indicated as being necessary conditions by a minority of children in the junior age range. No children mentioned sleep or rest.

**Table 4.20   Necessary Conditions for Caterpillar Growth:
Percentages by Age Group**

	Infant n = 18	Lower Juniors n = 24	Upper Juniors n = 18	All n = 60
Food; Cabbage, lettuce, etc.	33 (6)	42 (10)	72 (13)	48 (29)
Drink; juice, water, liquid, fluid etc.	-	8 (2)	17 (3)	8 (5)
Breath; air, oxygen, etc.	-	4 (1)	28 (5)	10 (6)
Warmth	-	-	11 (2)	3 (2)
Cool, shade	-	-	11 (2)	3 (2)
Sleep, rest	-	-	-	-

The overall number of conditions mentioned by each age group is summarised in
Table 4.21 which shows a steeper age gradient than was the case for observations
(Table 4.19).

**Table 4.21   Number of Conditions Identified as Necessary to Caterpillar
Growth; Percentages by Age   Group**

	Infant n = 18	Lower Juniors n = 24	Upper Juniors n = 18	All n = 60
None	72 (13)	50 (12)	28 (5)	50 (30)
One	22 (4)	38 (9)	22 (4)	28 (17)
Two	6 (1)	13 (3)	22 (4)	13 (8)
Three	-	-	28 (5)	8 (5)
Mean Number of Conditions Identified	0.3	0.6	1.5	0.8

p<0.01, chi square 18.3, d.f. = 6

The questioning used to elicit children's ideas about the mechanism of growth took its cue from the discussion about the conditions needed for growth summarised above. The conditions suggested by children were reflected back with the question, 'How does that help it to grow?' A further question was used to develop any ideas which were forthcoming : 'What do you think is happening inside the caterpillar to make it grow?' Responses to this area of questioning are summarised in Table 4.17.

**Table 4.22   Ideas About the Mechanism of Caterpillar Growth;
                Percentages by Age Group**

	Infant n = 18	Lower Juniors n = 24	Upper Juniors n = 18	All n = 60
'Food' makes it grow, no elaboration	17 (3)	13 (3)	17 (3)	15 (9)
Food makes it bigger/longer/fatter/ heavier	11 (2)	-	33 (6)	13 (8)
Food makes caterpillar *stretch*	-	-	17 (3)	5 (3)
Food is *digested*	-	-	11 (2)	3 (2)
Part of food is incorporated, part is passed out	-	-	-	-
Blood is moving, circulating	-	-	11 (2)	3 (2)
Strength is increased	-	-	17 (3)	5 (3)
Health is increased	-	4 (1)	-	2 (1)
Air makes it expand	-	-	2 (1)	2 (1)

Table 4.22 records the fact that no children offered a formal description of the mechanism of animal growth even at the simple molar level i.e. part of ingested food being incorporated, with waste material being excreted. The most common response, offered by one third of upper juniors (and eleven per cent of infants) attributed growth to food, but without specifying a detailed mechanism; food was simply recognised as being associated with an increase in mass/volume. Whether ingestion alone was regarded as a sufficient explanation is not certain, though further probing did not produce elaboration. The sufficiency of ingestion as a *mechanism* was explicit in those responses from upper juniors (17%) suggesting that taking in food actually caused the caterpillars to 'stretch', and this stretching was apparently seen as synonymous with growth.

> *"It's just a bit like stretching it a bit, making it go into a different shape."*

(Age 10 years)

5. INTERVENTION

The Pilot Elicitation phase enabled children to express a wide range of ideas about growth. This data enabled the Project team to gain an overview of the recurrent features in the children's ideas as well as some insight into the situations and experiences which had led to these ideas developing. The recurrent features in children's ideas about growth formed the basis for a range of Intervention strategies used by teachers in the classrooms.

It was thought that the chance of conceptual change might be enhanced by allowing children to work in the area that interested them most. For this reason, teachers were presented with the Intervention strategies and encouraged to develop classroom work particular to their own classes. It was felt that, in order to attempt to influence children's ideas, it would be beneficial for the teachers to focus the children's thoughts on one particular aspect of 'Growth', rather than try to cover everything in a superficial manner. It was also suggested that the main focus of the Intervention work should be encouraging children to test out their ideas - so that teachers were using the children's ideas as starting points for classroom activity. Teachers were asked to hold a minimum of four sessions based on Intervention work over the five-week Intervention period and to ensure they included at least one activity related to vocabulary, generalisations and trying out children's ideas. They were also asked to keep a record of the Intervention work they undertook, particularly in relation to the children who were to be re-interviewed after the work. Teachers received a visit from a member of the research team each week during this period in order that support and guidance might be offered. The guidelines given to teachers are in Appendix VI.

5.1 INTERVENTION STRATEGIES

The following paragraphs describe the Intervention strategies and the way that it was advocated that they could be approached during work on growth.

Helping children to test their own ideas

Children's ideas about plant and animal growth were often context-specific, based upon observations which had been made from a limited range of experiences. Plants, for example, were often thought to need soil in order to grow. The distinction between germination and growth could be problematic with regard to the need for soil: an idea suggesting that soil is always necessary at every stage of seed and plant growth could be tested and refined. By encouraging children to test their ideas in a rigorous manner it was envisaged that children's thinking might develop along lines which might be more productive. This strategy, of children testing their ideas, was the main focus of each class's Intervention experience.

Encouraging children to generalise from one specific context to others through discussion.

The context-specificity of children's ideas has already been mentioned. Teachers were asked to provide a forum, through class discussions, for children to share their ideas and experiences so that the class members could have access to a broader range of experiences. The opportunity for peer discussion might enable children to develop their ideas and link a wider range of experiences.

Encouraging children to develop more specific definitions for particular keywords.

Certain key words were either used incorrectly or not used at all. The word 'growing' was used with several meanings by children, for example, 'getting bigger', 'being pushed out by water' and 'getting longer'. There was also evidence of some confusion with 'stretching'. Teachers were asked to encourage children, through activities, to refine the definitions and to move towards a consensus meaning for some words which were central to the topic of growth.

Finding ways to make imperceptible change perceptible.

The rate of growth is so slow as to be imperceptible but the results of growth can easily be seen as an increase in size. The fact that 'growing' cannot be observed in the normal classroom situation is problematic to many children, particularly younger ones, and a resolution of the conundrum which was commonly constructed was that growth must occur while the child is absent. Teachers were asked to explore ways of making the very slow process of growth perceptible to children.

5.2 CLASSROOM IMPLEMENTATION OF THE INTERVENTION

The nature of the topic 'Growth' is such that certain ethical restrictions are placed upon investigative work that can be carried out. Because of this, the vast majority of classroom interventions were concerned with plant growth, and particularly the conditions necessary for broad beans to grow.

The following are some examples of interventions which were initiated by teachers with their classes:

Trying out children's ideas: 'What Do Plants Need To Grow?' (Middle Infants)

The teacher had decided to try to explore the notion, arising from imperceptible growth, that plants only grow at night. However, during the introductory discussion the children's responses were connected with conditions for plant growth, so this alternative avenue was pursued. The discussion began in a way familiar to the children, by recalling the previous Exploration experiences with broad beans. Children suggested that broad beans need mud (soil), sun and water to grow. When asked if it would be possible to grow the beans with any of the soil, sun or water missing, three children each volunteered one set of conditions:

> "Try it without mud"
> "Try it without water"
> "Try it without sun"

Four pots were set up by the children, one for each of the above conditions and one control, and three beans were put in each pot. The children suggested suitable locations for the four pots and were given the responsibility of caring for them. This investigation lasted for six weeks and, in the words of the class teacher, 'The children's interest never waned throughout the Intervention and the activities were looked at spontaneously every day without prompting.' When the 'no water' beans failed to grow the children were able to suggest adding water, and when the 'no sun' beans were found to have small, yellow leaves the class suggested putting the pot in the light. The children's investigations had given them experiences which they were able to interpret and use to extend and confirm their hypotheses.

Developing Vocabulary: 'What does 'Grow' Mean?' (First Year Juniors)

The children appeared to have defined the word 'grow' in terms of 'stretching' - increasing the length of something without adding any more material to it - and they often seemed to use the two terms synonymously, e.g.

> "I think when the plant is taking in water it is stretching the plant, stretching it from the seed as high as it can."

The teacher made a collection of articles which increased in size by either growing or stretching, e.g. Christmas decorations, bubbles, knitting, stocking, treacle toffee, springs, and the children stretched themselves during a movement lesson. The children were able, during discussion, to explain quite clearly that stretching needed help and could not go beyond a limit, that things would break if stretched beyond a certain point or would return to normal if let go. The definition of growth was still unclear; it was thought that knitting might grow, by adding more wool on, but that as it could be unravelled and animal or plant growth was permanent, they might not be the same. The children had clearly been stimulated to think carefully about the two words even though their conclusions were incomplete.

Generalisations and Making the Imperceptible Perceptible: 'When Does Growth Take Place?' (Fourth Year Juniors)

This class had successfully reared its batch of caterpillars and the teacher decided to capitalise on the children's interest and explore animal growth through discussion. A recurrent notion during the Exploration had been that the caterpillars grow at one particular time, e.g.

> *"While they're sleeping"*
> *"They grow when they eat"*
> *"They need darkness"*

The children were encouraged to consider parts of their own bodies which grew, e.g. hair, teeth and nails, and whether these obviously changed in length at any time, for example during a meal or overnight. This theme was pursued with the use of a video film illustrating metamorphosis through time-lapse photography. The time-lapse photography enabled gradual, continuous growth to be seen by increasing the rate of change. These two activities had the effect of provoking the children to consider their ideas concerning the caterpillars critically, and to relate the caterpillar growth to their own.

5.3 THE INTERACTION BETWEEN SCIENCE SKILLS AND SCIENCE CONCEPTS

The Intervention work raised some interesting and unexpected issues, as well as revealing the ingenuity of children and teachers alike. It was felt that, in order to influence concepts the main thrust of the teachers' interventions had to be through encouraging application of scientific processes to the children's investigations. This revealed a distinction between science concepts and processes which was problematic, with some teachers being reluctant to influence scientific rigour; they had become used to standing back and 'not telling' and were unsure whether or not to interfere in experimental design. The teacher meetings held throughout the Intervention (every two weeks) enabled teachers to share their work and discuss issues such as 'What is a generalization?'.

5.4 SUMMARY

It will be clear that, in view of the child-centred intervention strategies which were adopted, the interventions could not be said to be standardised to any precise degree. However, the strategies were common to all groups . Teachers were also asked to keep a careful record of their intervention activities.

The Project team developed a range of strategies for Intervention which teachers implemented in their classrooms. The starting points for the classroom work were the children's ideas.

The importance of controlling children's use of process skills during investigations became very evident during the Intervention.

The Intervention strategies were:

- Using children's ideas as the starting point of investigation

- Encouraging children to develop more specific definitions for particular key words.

- Encouraging children to generalize from one specific context to others through discussion.

- Finding way to make imperceptible changes perceptible.

6. OUTCOMES OF INTERVENTION

The Project's view of learning - that children construct their own knowledge and understanding of objects and events in the world - governed the way in which information about children's ideas was collected. Having established a baseline in terms of the range and frequencies of prevailing ideas, attention was turned to the issue of how these ideas might be developed or changed.

It was not the intention to point out to children that their ideas were wrong in those cases where they did not accord with scientific explanations. Nor was it the intention to expose them to 'the truth', in the manner of a model lesson. The constructivist view of learning implies that children are likely to make their own sense of whatever information they encounter, and that 'sense' is largely determined by how experience has influenced the way they look at the world. This assumption of an active and selective interpretation of experiences which they encounter would apply equally to their reception of a model lesson. Transmitted information, however carefully constructed, would be likely to be selectively filtered and distorted on receipt.

One of the major thrusts of the Intervention was to encourage children to explore actively the implications of their own ideas. In practice, this meant that they would investigate empirically what would otherwise be assertion. The implementation of this investigatory aspect was crucial to the project in several respects. It indicated a commitment to exploring the implications of the constructivist view of learning beyond collecting examples of interesting ideas. It broke new ground in terms of acknowledging in practice the relationship between concept development and the process skills of science. For teachers, it relieved the anxiety which 'standing off' caused them, when children voiced their misconceptions. At this point teachers were able to say to children,

"How would you investigate whether what you have said is correct? How would you find out? What would you look for? What would you measure? How would you make sure your test was a fair one?" And so on.

The dilemma of being a teacher but not allowed to teach was resolved, and the anxiety was relieved. The pressure was now on the teacher to adopt a quite different role, as a manager of children's learning, with the onus for the justification of ideas being subtly transferred to the children who expressed them.

For many teachers, probably the majority, possibly all of them, the project had introduced a novel view of learning; certainly novel in the sense of developing and exploring the implications of that view for classroom practice. The major classroom implication was the radical change in teaching practice which it implied for some teachers.

into a consideration of teachers' needs: needs in relation to understanding the science concepts involved; needs in respect of the process of scientific investigations; needs in terms of managing pupil-centred learning.

The above catalogue of issues must be appreciated when evaluating the outcomes of Intervention. Teachers had not anticipated at the outset the radical implications of the research programme for their own practice; they accommodated the demands to varying degrees. Some teachers found the implications very difficult to accommodate within their existing mode of practice; some found things difficult but contributed hard-earned insights to the debate; to others, the programme was a revelation. This latter group really took hold of the project and developed their thinking and practice. Their enthusiasm and that of the children in their classes was self-evident.

Clearly the quality of children's investigations was variable and consequently, to look for changes in the group as a whole is a most stringent criterion with which to evaluate the intervention programme. More realistically, changes in teachers' practice which could improve the quality and rigour of children's investigations is an essential prior condition.

The Project team was fairly confident that it witnessed changes in teachers' practice, changes in teachers' and children's attitudes and an increased motivation and sense of competence in relation to science. These aspects of development were not quantified, (though they are recorded in teachers' own records of their work) but are the essential foundations which underpin any development in children's thinking.

The particular focus of attention which teachers were encouraged to develop in the Intervention was children's ideas about plant growth, using the broad bean. Investigations tended to relate to the conditions in which growth occurred. Table 6.1. summarises children's responses as categorised from the pre- and post-Intervention interviews.

Table 6.1   **Suggested Conditions Necessary for Growth of Broad Bean, Pre- and Post-Intervention; Percentages by Age Group.**

	Pre-Intervention			Post-Intervention		
	Inf. (n=20)	L.J. (n=24)	U.J. (n=18)	Inf. (n=13)	L.J. (n=15)	U.J. (n=14)
Air[1]	-	-	22 (4)	-	20 (3)	14 (2)
Oxygen	-	-	11 (2)	-	-	-
Carbon Dioxide	-	-	-	-	-	-
Sun	25 (5)	21 (5)	22 (4)	31 (4)	13 (2)	36 (5)
Light	5 (1)	8 (2)	22 (4)	15 (2)	67 (10)	36 (5)
Warmth/Heat	5 (1)	13 (3)	39 (7)	-	7 (1)	29 (4)
Water/moisture/ damp	85 (17)	100 (24)	83 (15)	85 (11)	93 (14)	93 (13)
Soil/compost/sand	30 (6)	29 (7)	56 (10)	39 (5)	53 (8)	36 (5)
Plant food/minerals/ fertiliser	5 (1)	4 (1)	11 (2)	8 (1)	13 (2)	21 (3)
Soil cover	-	-	6 (1)	-	-	7 (1)
Creatures (in or above soil)	-	4 (1)	6 (1)	-	7 (1)	-
Darkness	-	8 (2)	11 (2)	8 (1)	13 (2)	-
Cool	-	4 (1)	6 (1)	-	-	7 (1)
The bean/roots/ leaves (tautology)	20 (4)	4 (1)	6 (1)	8 (1)	7 (1)	-

[1] Some children suggested more than one condition.

Responses relating to 'sun' and 'light' are of particular interest. It was suggested earlier (p. 49) that a reference to 'light' might be a more differentiated observation than to 'sun'. In the pre-Intervention sample, the gradient of increasing reference to light with increasing age was noted. It is most encouraging to see that, post-intervention, references to light have increased almost four-fold in the sample as a whole. This is an important shift. It indicates a more precise observation. It advances children towards an appreciation of the critical function of light in the process of photosynthesis. It is also indicating an awareness of how a perceptible but intangible variable has a major part to play in the process of growth. The frequency of reference to light was actually greater in the lower junior than upper junior sample, post-Intervention, which might be evidence to suggest that greater shifts are possible.

The other variable which shows some positive change is the condition of soil/plant food. The frequency of references to plant food/minerals/fertiliser doubled, with the age gradient maintained.

Table 6.2 summarises in more general terms how children's perception of the conditions necessary for growth changed. The mean number of conditions suggested (omitting tautological comments) shows an increase for all age groups, with a particularly large jump for the lower juniors.

Table 6.2 Broad Bean in Soil: Number of Conditions Identified as Helpful for Growth, Pre- and Post -Intervention; Percentages by Age Group

	Pre-Intervention				Post-Intervention			
	Inf. (n=20)	L.J. (n=24)	U.J. (n=18)	All (n=62)	Inf. (n=13)	L.J. (n=15)	U.J. (n=14)	All (n=42)
Number of Conditions Identified								
None	10 (2)	-	-	3 (2)	-	-	-	-
One	40 (8)	29 (7)	-	24 (15)	39 (5)	20 (3)	-	19 (8)
Two	40 (8)	54 (13)	22 (4)	40 (25)	23 (3)	7 (1)	43 (6)	24 (10)
Three	10 (2)	13 (3)	67 (12)	27 (17)	38 (5)	40 (6)	36 (5)	38 (16)
Four	-	4 (1)	11 (2)	5 (3)	-	27 (4)	14 (2)	14 (6)
Five	-	-	-	-	-	7 (1)	7 (1)	5 (1)
Mean Number of Conditions Identified	1.5	1.9	2.8	2.1	2.0	2.9	2.9	2.6

These increases are probably attributable to the more focussed observations which were encouraged. More detailed and more reflective comments seemed to emerge as a result.

Children were also asked about the source of new plant material and pre- and post-Intervention responses are summarised in Table 6.3. Insufficient responses from infants were available to warrant inclusion in Table 6.3, which summarises responses for junior-age children only.

Perhaps the greatest interest of Table 6.3 is that it indicates that certain changes did not occur. The vast majority of children still attributed the production of new material to the bean itself, but more explicitly to sources or mechanisms inside the bean. Interviewers were possibly sensitised to this issue as the result of pre-Intervention interviews and sought more precise clarification from children.

Teasing out children's ideas about the sources of new plant material required fairly persistent questioning to clarify their exact understanding. The following interview transcript indicates an understanding that new materials had been incorporated. It was conducted while the child actually handled an uprooted bean (of about 10 cm in height) which had been grown in the class.

Transcript 6.1

Q.   If we'd taken one of the broad beans and weighed it at the beginning, and then we weighed the plant it grew into - we washed the soil off, and everything - and we weighed the plant and compared the two, what would we have found?

R.   *The plant would be heavier.*

Q.   Why would that be?

R.   *Because it's grown more, it's got leaves and that growing from it, made some weight.*

Q.   You say it's 'made some weight'. What do you mean by that?

R.   *It's like when you have no plant, it was the same weight and when you weighed it with the plant it goes heavier because it's got more stuff.*

Q.   ' It's got more stuff '. What is that stuff that it's got?

R.   *A stem and leaves.*

Q.   But where has the extra weight come from?

R.   *It's come from the water which when it sucks it in, you know, on the plant, when the water goes in, the plant grows a little bit to take it like full up, and then it comes out."*

Q.   What do you mean, ' it comes out? '

R.   *Like, it had water in and some little bits came popping out.*

Q.   Some little bits came popping out where?

R.   *From the top of the bean.*

Q.   And what would they look like?

R.   *Small little stems.*

Some responses left no doubt that children were still of the view that all growth had unfolded from the bean itself. Given a similar context to the interview above, the following three children offered very different ideas.

Transcript 6.2

Q.   ".........how would the weight of the plant compare with the weight of the broad bean?"

R.   *"I think it would be the same again."*

Q.   "Why do you think it would be the same?"

R.   *"Because at first we weighed the broad bean and then we weighed it again - I think it would still be the same because the seed grew into it, a plant."*

(Age 11 years)

Transcript 6.3

Q.   "......what do you think we would find about the weight?"

R.   *"The plant would be bigger because it had grown full really high."*

Q.   "Yes. And how would the weight compare with when it was a bean?"

R.   *"I don't know."*

Q.   (gently) "What would you think?"

R.   *"The first bean, when it wasn't grown, might have been a bit heavier because all the plant was inside it, and all the stalk."*

(Age 10 years)

Transcript 6.4

Q.   "......what would we find if we compare the weight of those two? (i.e. plant and bean)

R.   *"If we weigh it the first time, it would have been heavier, and if we weigh it afterwards, it would have been lighter.*

Q.   The bean will be heavier than the plant?

R.   *Yes.*

Q.   How do you explain that?

R.   *Because when it was full of bean it was heavier because it had all its things inside it and afterwards everything would have split up and things would have dropped off it.*

Q.   When it was a plant?

R.   *Yes.*

Q.   Things would have dropped off it?

R.   *Yes. Like the roots. Some fall off.*

Q.   So where does all that stuff that makes the plant - where does all that come from - all the leaves and all the stems and all the roots?

R.   *Inside the bean.*

Q.   It comes from inside the bean, you think?

R.   *Some might come from the soil.*

(Age 10 years)

Because the idea in the above transcript was articulated with startling clarity, the child was invited to repeat it. When the idea was reflected back a second time, either in response to the interviewer's reaction or as the result of being pressed to reflect, some doubt perhaps crept into the child's mind. This illustrates the fact that all interactions, including data-collection interviews, contribute to the dynamic of change. It would be misleading to portray children's ideas in any other way - like pinned butterflies in a show-case, for example. Nevertherless, the dialogue is evidence of some clear ideas about growth which make no reference to the incorporation of new material and perhaps supports the interpretation of Table 6.3.

Table 6.3 **Broad Bean in Soil; Sources of New Plant Material, Pre- and Post-Intervention; Percentages by Age Group.**

	Pre-Intervention			Post-Intervention		
	L.J. n = 22	U.J. n = 17	All n = 39	L.J. n = 11	U.J. n = 14	All n = 25
Reference to Materials Inside the Bean						
From the bean	18 (4)	12 (2)	15 (6)	-	-	-
From *inside* the bean	59 (13)	59 (10)	59 (23)	82 (9)	79 (11)	80 (20)
The stem from the bean, the leaves from the stem/shoots	14 (3)	24 (4)	18 (7)	9 (1)	-	5 (1)
Reference to Materials outside Bean being incorporated						
Reference to soil/ minerals/compost	-	6 (1)	3 (1)	-	14 (2)	8 (2)
Reference to water/ moisture	-	6 (1)	3 (1)	-	36 (5)	20 (5)
Reference to air/ gases	-	6 (1)	3 (1)	-	-	-
Other	-	-	-	-	7 (1)	4 (1)
Don't know	5 (1)	-	3 (1)	9 (1)	-	4 (1)
No response	5 (1)	-	3 (1)	-	-	-

There was an increase in the frequency of recognition of incorporation of materials from outside the bean, particularly water. All the incorporation responses came from upper juniors; the shift within the age group was from 6% to 36%. It could be that children's relative willingness to accept the idea of the incorporation of water is the point at which the erroneous notion of a growing plant as a closed system is most likely to be breached.

Table 6.4 summarises ideas about the mechanism of germination and growth, pre- and post-Intervention. The availability of post-Intervention interview data was limited to responses from three infants, nine lower juniors and seven upper juniors. While whole group comparisons are not equivalent in age composition, pre- and post-Intervention data are sufficiently interesting to warrant summarising and reporting.

Table 6.4   Broad Bean in Soil: The Mechanism of Germination and Growth; Pre- and Post-Intervention; Percentages

	Pre-Intervention n=49	Post-Intervention n=19
Reforming/reorganisation of materials	4 (2)	42 (8)
Enlargement; increase in mass/ volume/size	27 (13)	16 (3)
Growth/growing	18 (9)	11 (2)
Water enlarges/softens/swells the bean, is taken in/enters	39 (19)	74 (14)
Roots/shoots push or exert force	18 (9)	11 (2)
Straightening, uncurling	12 (6)	11 (2)
Seed within a seed	6 (3)	5 (1)
Increase in 'strength' of plant	8 (4)	16 (3)
Other mechanisms	8 (4)	5 (1)

The most dramatic increase is in the number of children expressing some notion of reforming or re-organisation of material within the bean. Less dramatic, but still considerable, is the number of children identifying water as having some part to play in the process of germination and growth. As part of their investigational work, many children were encouraged to dissect the broad bean seeds. It may be speculated that those who held a notion of growth as an ufurling of the folded material inside the seed may have encountered a perceptible challenge and consequent disequilibrium when a relatively homongeneous interior was revealed. Thus it is consistent that a number of children shifted their ideas towards accepting that an internal *reforming* or *reorganisation* of materials must take place, without necessarily taking on the notion of the reorganisation of *incorporated* materials in the formation of the plant.

Transcript 6.5

(Pre-Intervention)

Q.   What do you think is happening inside the bean?

R.   *Very thin root-like shoots grow up and push through the top, out through the black bit.*

(Post-Intervention)

Q.   What do you think is happening inside the bean?

R.   *There's loads of shells inside each other. They must change into the leaves and shoot because we cut one open and it was empty.*

'Empty' presumably, in the sense of the expected curled up plant not being found and the inside of the seed being observed to be relatively undifferentiated. The simple strategy of allowing children to see with their own eyes is a potentially powerfully influential challenge to their thinking. This is especially so when, as appeared to be the case, the majority of children had little direct experience of seeds of the plant species which they ate daily. Teachers may need to overcome what might be a reluctance to dissect seeds and uproot plants during the process of growth in order to make these experiences accessible to children. No doubt children would also benefit from similar revelations in relation to animal growth, but using secondary sources in parallel with their direct experiences, for obvious ethical reasons.

Post-Intervention interview data about when growth occurs was available for 25 children, comprising five infants, nine lower juniors and eleven upper juniors. The major change noted after the Intervention activities was the increase in the frequency of responses describing growth as continuous.

Table 6.5   **Broad Bean in Soil: Ideas About When Growth Occurs; Pre- and Post-Intervention; Percentages by Age Group**

	Pre-Intervention n=62	Post-Intervention n=25
Continuously, little by little, day and night	35 (22)	56 (14)
During the day/morning	11 (7)	4 (1)
At night	15 (9)	20 (5)
Related to Seasons/Calendar	13 (8)	4 (1)
When external conditions are suitable (e.g. food/water available)	15 (9)	12 (3)
In pupils' absence	3 (2)	-
Other	3 (2)	-
Don't know	5 (3)	4 (1)
Totals	100 (62)	100 (25)

Although not a large shift, once again this is in the right direction; all such responses were from children of junior age, six (67% of the 9 interviewed) lower juniors, eight (72% of the 11 interviewed) upper juniors.

Transcript 6.6

Q.   So when do you think plants do their growing?

R.   *They are growing all the time. I think so.*

Q.   What about you? When do you do your growing?

R.   *When I'm asleep.*

Q.   So people are different from plants, are they?

R.   *Well, not really, I don't think. We still need food and water.*

Q.   But we grow at different times, you're suggesting?

R.   *Yes.*

Q.   Is there any way you could test that idea?

R.   *You would measure a plant and measure us and then see if we had grown and see if the plant had grown.*

Q.   At different times?

R.   *Yes.*

Q.   Now, you told me that your grandfather had some ideas about when people grow. (Reference to the previous interview)

R.   *Yes. You see, we got that one because we were in our room and I said, 'When will I be able to drive my tractor?' because I drive one but my grandad is nearly always there, but not for doing field work. And he said, 'When you've grown a bit', and I said, 'How do I do that?', and he said, 'Well, keep hiccoughing and you'll grow'.*

Q.   Do you think he really believes that?

R.   *I don't know.*

Q.   Do you believe it?

R.   *No, not really.*

Q.   I thought you did believe it when you told me, last time.

R.   *Well, I did, but I've changed my mind.*

Q.   Did you ask him about it?

R.   *No.*

Q.   What's made you change your mind?

R.   *Well, I suppose, my friend, He's small and he hiccoughs nearly all the time. He hasn't grown.*

(Age 10 years)

As well as illustrating the conviction with which beliefs summarised in Table 6.4 may be held, Transcript 6.6 is also a reminder that there are many influences on children's beliefs beyond the classrooms walls, not least grandads and other sources of folklore.

7. SUMMARY

The wider implications of a project concerned with the apparently straightforward task of identification and changing of children's ideas in a classroom context are perhaps revealed in this report on work in the area of children's understanding of growth. Many wider issues relating to teachers and pupils are linked inextricably in such a programme. Consequently, the central core of activity, with its pre- and post-test design around a period of classroom Intervention, should be viewed as just one of the several kinds of change upon which the efficacy of the project must be judged. Since the pre- and post-intervention interviews were the major source of quantified data, the Project team harboured some apprehension that such a stringent criterion might reveal little of the qualitative changes which could be more overtly perceived. In the event, data revealed some measurable quantitative changes also, and this is a bonus. The ideas expressed by children and quoted in the body of the report give some indication of their involvement and commitment and their willingness to struggle with ideas and their expression. Some broad points emerging from the research can be summarised at this point.

7.1 SUMMARY OF SOME IMPORTANT IDEAS EMERGING FROM PRE-INTERVENTION INTERVIEWS

Germination and Growth of Broad Beans

From the classroom work it appeared that individual infants mentioned as conditions necessary for growth of the boad bean only water, sun and soil. (Very few mentioned all three). When soil was mentioned, it tended to be regarded as a support for the plant rather than a source of nutrients. Juniors mentioned water, soil and sun, but additionally, some differentiated light and heat; a few mentioned air or gases; soil was also recognised as providing nutrients by a small number of children.

Individual interviews revealed that the majority of children - infants and juniors - were of the view that the new plant material emerged from the bean seed. To an extent, this view might have been encouraged by the focus on germination as well as growth. There is no doubting the fact that many children see plant growth as an 'unfolding' of material, and to some, growth also seems to imply the generation of new material. Very few suggestions about incorporation of new material were encountered. A few, 40-50%, of juniors associated water with the *mechanism* of growth. About one quarter of juniors suggested that growth occurs at night time; older children revealed an increasing awareness of the span and limits of plant growth.

Growth of Mung Beans

Similar ideas were expressed in relation to the growth of mung beans (growth in a dark, moist environment). Almost all children appreciated that the presence of water was a necessary condition for the growth of mung beans, yet this was as an external facilitator rather than something which becomes part of the fabric of the bean or part of the process of growth. The fact that the mung beans were grown in the dark was not associated with an increased frequency of responses suggesting that growth occurs at night-time.

Growth Inside Eggs

Classroom work on growth within the assumed closed-system of the egg revealed four main ideas about development:

- the incubation period was assumed to be the time when complete body parts came together inside the egg. This idea was not very frequently expressed.

- some children considered that the complete animal was simply inside the egg waiting to hatch.

- a majority of children suggested that a structurally complete but miniature animal was feeding on the support system within the egg.

- a minority of children suggested some transformation of the contents of the egg into a structurally refined animal.

Some children attempted to differentiate the function of yolk and white in the hen's egg; for most children, these were described as providing food and drink, respectively.

Some explanations of what was happening inside the egg drew on other sources of knowledge, particularly human foetal development. There were references to the chick or caterpillar kicking or moving inside the egg and emerging without sight being developed.

It was not unusual to find that children made assumptions about growth inside the egg being associated with increases in mass *within* the system, i.e. that the process of growth generated new material.

Individual Interviews relating to the eggs of the Cabbage White butterfly confirmed that ideas about the reorganisation and transformation of material occurred infrequently. Food was the most commonly recognised requirement inside the egg; drink, warmth, and protection were each mentioned by about one sixth of upper juniors. Air or oxygen was mentioned by about one quarter of upper juniors. Assumptions of an overall increase in mass of the egg resulting from the growth of the caterpillar inside it were not uncommon.

Caterpillar Growth

Children's observations relating to the growth of caterpillars omitted some very obvious features - especially the production of droppings. Food, drink, air, warmth and (cool) shade were identified as necessary conditions. No children offered anything like a conventional biological explanation of animal growth involving incorporation and transformation of material. Ingestion seemed to be regarded as a sufficient explanation, though this was sometimes elaborated to include the idea of stretching.

7.2 CHANGES IN FREQUENCIES OF RESPONSE, POST-INTERVENTION

References to light as a necessary condition for plant growth were noted pre-Intervention with increasing frequency with age; overall, the increase in reference to light was three-to-four-fold, post-Intervention. 'Light' appears to be a more differentiated response than 'sun', as a necessary condition for growth.

The mean number of conditions posited as necessary for growth increased; references to soil or plant food doubled overall, post-Intervention.

Post-Intervention, the majority of the junior sample was still attributing the production of new material to the bean itself. There was an increase in the proportion of children referring to the incorporation of material, particularly water. All 'incorporation' responses came from upper juniors, the shift within the age group being from 6% to 36%.

There was an increase in the proportion of children referring to a reforming or reorganisation of materials within the bean, post-Intervention. (Dissection of beans may have helped.) The number of children identifying water as having some part to play in the process of germination and growth increased substantially.

Post-Intervention, more children described growth as a continuous process.

7.3 TECHNIQUES AS PRODUCTS

The close collaboration between researchers and teachers proved to be extremely productive in testing and refining a range of techniques, both for elicitation of ideas and for intervention. These techniques have a currency beyond research uses. The elicitation techniques included a novel development of log-books from diaries as a manageable form of pupil-directed record-keeping of the emergence and development of ideas. *Drawings of ideas* as a medium of expression, proved to be another extremely useful technique. Drawing was found especially valuable in view of the duration of the process of growth, where records and projections of expected growth were particularly valuable. The Intervention experiences also helped to forge new techniques, or to explore new angles on existing ones.

7.4 UNDERSTANDING TEACHERS' NEEDS

A realisation of teachers' needs in relation to the teaching of science in primary schools was another area which was greatly clarified by the research. Three areas can be identified:-

(a)   Conceptual understanding. Teachers' own understanding of the processes of plant and animal growth undoubtedly broadened and deepened during the course of the project.

(b)   An understanding of process-based science was essential for the Intervention phase. For many teachers, their competence and experience in other areas of the curriculum did not provide solutions which generalised to science.

(c)   Combining (a) and (b) above, a style of teaching is suggested which can best be described as a teacher-directed, pupil-centred, management of learning. This was in direct contrast to the assumption which many teachers held that science was pre-eminently about the transmission of knowledge - especially so in the context of a research project about conceptual development.

As the project has progressed, there has been a notable increase in the confidence of many of the teachers, not just in their attitude towards the project but also in the manner in which they approach their classes. This attitude is in many cases not restricted to science work, since teachers have become more aware of the manner in which they may enable children to learn, and also of what children bring with them to the classroom situation. As one teacher summarised her experience,

'The amount of information the children had acquired without being taught per se amazed me, and I was convinced that involvement, observation and experience were invaluable methods of learning.'

BIBLIOGRAPHY

BARKER, M.A.B. (1986). *The Description and Modification of Children's Views of Plant Nutrition.* University of Waikato.

BELL, B., BROOK, A. (1984). *Aspects of Secondary Students' Understanding of Plant Nutrition.* Full Report. CLIS: Childrens' Learning in Science Project. Centre for Studies in Science and Mathematics Education. The University of Leeds.

BELL., B., BROOK, A. (1984). *Aspects of Secondary Students' Understanding of Plant Nutrition.* Summary Report. CLIS: Childrens' Learning in Science Project. Centre for Studies in Science and Mathematics Education. The University of Leeds.

BELL, B. (1985). Students' ideas about plant nutrition : what are they? *Journal of Biological Education*, 19(3), 213-218.

SCHAEFER, J.P., SCHMIDT FRENCH, B. (1986). *Teaching and Learning Genetics : A Case Studies of academic Work in Two Classrooms.* Paper presented at the annual meeting of the American Education Research Association, San Francisco, April.

APPENDIX I

SPACE SCHOOL PERSONNEL

LANCASHIRE

County Adviser for Science: Mr P Garner

School	Head Teacher	Teachers
Moor Nook Primary	Mr G Robinson	Mrs M Harrison Mrs L McGuigan
Farington Primary	Mr P S Warren	Mr J Evans Mrs M Pearce
St Teresa's RC Primary	Mr L Rigby	Mrs A Hall Mrs R Morton
Frenchwood Primary	Miss E M Cowell	Mrs L Bibby Mrs C Pickering
Clough Fold Primary	Mr G M Horne	Mrs J Looker Mrs C Murray
Longton Junior	Mr J R Doran	Miss R Hamm Mrs L Whitby

APPENDIX II

Teacher pack for Exploration 1 (March 1987)

PRIMARY
SCIENCE PROCESSES AND CONCEPT EXPLORATION
PROJECT

The SPACE project is funded by the Nuffield Foundation and is run jointly by Liverpool University, Centre for Research in Primary Science and Technology, and Kings College, London (KQC), Centre for Educational Studies.

The long term aims of this project are to influence the teaching of science concepts in primary schools. Certain key science concepts have been selected, and the initial task will be to establish what ideas children hold in these areas. Conversations with children often show that they try to make sense of the world around them by generalising from their own experiences. In this way, they develop coherent ideas which they use to explain things in their environment. However, these notions may be scientifically inaccurate and may actually hinder later formal learning of scientific concepts.

Talking to children will be centrally important in discovering what beliefs they hold in the chosen concept areas. Exposing the children to examples of a concept without giving any factual input should encourage them to think about the area. A variety of techniques, formal and informal, conducted in groups or individually, will then be used to explore their ideas.

Having explored children's informal ideas, the next step will be to consider ways of modifying them in the desired direction. The knowledge accumulated about children's starting points will form the basis for intervention. Children will be encouraged to test commonly recurring misconceptions during their own investigations. It remains to be seen whether children's ideas will be modified when they actively apply science processes in the chosen topic areas.

The flow chart on the opposite page details the activities which are envisaged up until December 1988.

FLOW CHART

Sept. to Dec.	1986	Detailed arrangements made with LEAs. Teachers identified; schools selected. Initial draft of concept list drawn up by project directors. Concept areas identified and initial tasks defined.
Jan 1st to Feb.	1987	Full-time researcher appointed. Meetings with teacher groups for discussion of draft concept list and assignment of activities.
March	1987	Teachers collect data using agreed activities.
April to May	1987	Data analysed by team.
June	1987	Evidence shared with teachers leading to suggestions of strategies for changing children's ideas. Teachers' opinions surveyed for the evaluation. Teachers prepare materials for activities for new class.
Sept. to Dec.	1987	Teachers present activities as before to children and collect information about existing ideas - this constitutes pre-intervention evaluation data. Follow up with teaching involving the intervention strategies agreed. Children's responses to application activities collected - this provides the post-intervention evaluation data. Teachers' opinions surveyed.
Jan. to Feb.	1988	Work on new concept areas begins and data collected - pre-intervention data on children (as in March 1987).
March	1988	Data analysed by team.
April to May	1988	Evidence to teachers, intervention proposed and implemented. Teachers' opinions surveyed.
June to July	1988	Children's responses to application activities collected. Post-intervention data on some pupils. Teachers' opinions also collected.
Sept. to Dec.	1988	Data interpretation and report writing.

DATA COLLECTION PROPOSALS

Useful information about children's concepts can be obtained in each of the following settings:

1. Class activities
2. Group activities within a class setting
3. Individual interviews

1. <u>Class activities</u>

(a) These background activities are set up by the teachers and are designed to expose children to the concept area under exploration. It is important that each class in a topic group covers the same activities.

(b) Each activity involves a change which occurs over a period of time.

(c) The activity is set up in a convenient place, either in the classroom or in a corridor area.

(d) The children are encouraged to make careful observations and record anything they notice in a 'diary', starting with an initial description. The 'diary' can take the form of writing and/or pictures, and observations should be at regular intervals. The time interval between observations will obviously depend on the activity, e.g.:

> steel wool rusting - every 15 minutes initially
> plants growing - every day
> stick insects growing - once a week.

The children should not be led or directed in their interpretation of any changes, but encouraged to be as full as possible.

(e) A concluding, tape-recorded discussion is made to find out the children's ideas about the concepts involved in the activity. All questions which are asked by the teacher should be open and non-directing. Teachers will be asked to summarise the ideas emerging from these discussions. These summaries and labelled tapes should be kept in the buff folders.

2. <u>Group activities</u>

(a)   These activities develop the ideas initiated in the background activities. They maybe conducted by the teacher in a way which is compatible with the classroom organisation.

       Either i. the whole class working in groups at the same time
       or   ii. small groups working independently.

The teacher might also enlist the support of a group co-ordinator, research co-ordinator, or Head Teacher in conducting these group sessions. A written record or summary of ideas will be required.

(b)   The children in a group might jointly record each activity in a relevant form, i.e. diagram, list, written account.

(c)   The concluding discussion (1.(e)) is likely to tie in with the group activity since the group tasks focus on the change which has occurred.

3.   Individual interviews

(a)   These interviews focus on particular instances of the concept area under exploration. The orientation will have been provided by

          i.   a class or group activity
          ii.   assumed everyday experience
          iii.   a physical phenomenon or event based around (i) or (ii).

(b)   They are conducted by either the teacher, head teacher, group co-ordinator or research co-ordinator, as available.

(c)   The timing of the interview may coincide with the group activity or it may take place later, depending on the manpower available.

(d)   Selection of children for interviewing will be on the basis of:

          i.   ideas produced in the group/class activities;
          ii.   approximately equal numbers of each sex.

(e)   The number of children it will be possible to interview in detail will be determined by the duration of the interviews undertaken. Each group will need to make its own plans in consultation with the co-ordinators. The selection may be made by the teacher, head teacher or a co-ordinator.

(f)   Each topic group of schools should provide at least 20 interviews per concept area for each year group, i.e.:

10 1st year interviews about evaporation;
10 1st year interviews about condensation
and the same for infants, 2nd, 3rd, 4th year juniors.

This may involve teachers/group co-ordinators in setting up materials in additional classes in the school, or placing them in an area accessible to other children, e.g. a corridor.

(g)   The interviewer will record the child's ideas during the discussion with them, either by direct transcription or by later transcription if using an audio tape.

Data Collection

Any written material produced should be marked clearly with the date, the child's name (and sex if this is not obvious) and their year group. It should be kept in the buff folder.

INTERVIEWING TECHNIQUES

1. In order to explore children's own concepts it is important that their ideas should not have been influenced by teacher input. It is also important that the interviewer has no preconception about the content of the child's responses.

2. The child must be aware of the purpose of the interview, which is to establish the child's ideas about a particular topic. It must also be clear to the child that the interview is being recorded, either by transcription or on audio tape.

3. The interview questions in the topic pack are there as a guideline. One question may be enough stimulus for a whole interview. It may be more informative to follow the child's line of thinking than to try and go through the questions from beginning to end.

4. Any questions should be non-directive. They should be phrased so that the child can give any answer they feel is appropriate,

    e.g. "Tell me what you know about clouds"

5. The child should be allowed to talk freely, and the interviewer's attention given to picking up any critical words or phrases. These remarks can then form the basis of further questions which might focus more closely on the child's ideas.

    e.g. "We have to wash the beans twice a day because they need
           water or they'll shrivel up."

    "Can you tell me why you think the beans need water?"

6. The child should be encouraged to expand any answer they give, even if they appear to have contradicted previous statements. A look which registers the interviewer's surprise may inhibit the child's elaboration.

7. The questions should require no factual knowledge on the part of the child.

    e.g. "What is the name of this plant?"

    is not saying anything about the child's conceptual knowledge of plant growth.

    "What can you tell me about this plant?"

    might elicit the same information and also allow for other ideas to be put forward.

8. Questions with a yes/no answer should be avoided because they do not allow a free response.

    e.g. "Do you think the glass is cold?"

could be better phrased as:

"Have you any ideas why this happens to the glass?"

9.   It is a good idea to repeat what the child has said to make sure:

(a)   that they have said what they meant;

(b)   that their intended meaning is what has been understood.

Recapping may also prompt the child to elaborate their answer.

10.   It is possible that the interviewer and the child may use the same word to mean different things. It is necessary to ensure that the child's everyday meaning is understood.

11.   The length of the interview will obviously vary both with the subject matter and the child. It is important, though, that the discussion is not extended beyond its natural time limit in the hope of obtaining new ideas.

12.   During the course of an interview, children may change their minds. When this happens, all the ideas expressed should be recorded, in sequence. The temptation to summarise the discussion in terms of the final idea expressed will give a false impression of commitment or certainty, and should be avoided.

13.   All the above points stress the non-directive nature of the data collection. At the same time, interviewers must keep in mind the focus of interest of the interviews. This means:

(a)   all the points of interest to the topic are covered;

(b)   not too much time should be spent drifting into interesting but non-focal areas.

KIT LIST

GROWTH

Audio tapes
Cassette recorder
Paper - diaries
Yogurt pots
Large jam jars
Trays
Cotton wool
Paper towels
Seeds   -   maize
                mung beans
                broad beans
Soil
Potato tubers
Carrot tops
Dishes/saucers
Metre rulers
Tape measures
Rulers
Scales
Baby/puppy/kitten
Stick insects
Ivy/privet
Plants   -   spider plant
                strawberry
                varied pot plants
Trees
Mirrors
Photographs of selves
Incubators
Fertilized hens' eggs
Candler
Graph paper - mm square
                1 cm square
Flat containers to grow seeds in
Water
Paper - diaries

CLASS AND GROUP ACTIVITIES

These activities are ordered in terms of priority. Each school should agree to cover the same activities.

Plants

1. Potato

    Kit: potatoes
            diaries

Leave potatoes which are developing eyes to sprout.
Keep a diary of any observed changes.

Preparation: Leave in the dark for at least 3 weeks.

Group

(a)   Look at sprouting and non-sprouting potatoes.

(b)   List the similarities and differences between the tubers (or draw pictures and label the differences).

Discussion

(a)   What do you think is coming out of the potato?

(b)   What do you think is happening inside the potato?

(c)   Why do you think this is happening to the potato?

(d)   Do you think the potato plant will go on growing?

(e)   Can you think of anything else that this happens to?

2.   Bean Sprouts

    Kit: mung beans

large jam jar
diaries

Preparation: Soak the beans in a jar until the green casing begins to split (1 - 2 days). Pour off the water, rinse the seeds and drain them. Lay the jar on its side in a warm, dark place with the seeds spread out. Repeat the rinsing and draining until the sprouts are fully developed (approx. 12 days from starting soaking, so Monday is probably the best day to start).

3. Maize

Kit: yogurt pot
soil
jam jar
paper towel
cotton wool
diaries

Preparation: Soak overnight until they are swollen. Bend a paper towel round the inside of the jar. Fill the hole in the middle with cotton wool. The peas should be put halfway down the jar, between the glass and the paper towel. Put in with flat, white end downwards.

(a) In soil - visible growth in 12 - 14 days.

(b) In a glass jar - visible growth in 12 - 14 days.

Monitor the growth of the seedlings by marking a stick in the soil or drawing in crayon on the glass (both root and shoot).

4. Broad Beans

Kit: cotton wool
trays
broad beans
diaries

Preparation: soak overnight until they are swollen. Place in trays on top of cotton wool and cover with a damp cloth. Visible growth in 4 - 5 days.

Discussion

(a) What do you think is happening inside the seed?

(b)   Do you think the seed needs anything to make it grow?

(c)   What do you think the broad bean plant needs to make it grow?

(d)   Do you think the seedling will go on growing in the jar if we keep on looking after it?

Animals

1.   <u>Stick Insects</u>

Introduction

Stick insects live for about nine months. During this time they grow a great deal in length, shedding their skin at intervals. When fully grown they lay many eggs before dying. They feed on privet or ivy. They are best kept in a shady position at a normal room temperature. The eggs hatch in 3-4 months.

Setting up

1.   Use a large glass jar, small fish tank or a plastic margarine box.

2.   Put a piece of paper across the bottom to ease cleaning.

3.   Put in a few sprigs of ivy or privet in a small pot of water (preferably with a narrow opening to prevent insects drowning).

4.   Put the stick insects onto the leaves.

5.   Cover the jar with a piece of muslin secured with an elastic band.

Routine Maintenance

1.   When the stick insects have eaten all of the leaves (approx. weekly) remove everything from the jar.

2.   Put in a clean piece of paper and fresh ivy/privet.

3.   Check the old ivy/privet twigs for cast-off skins, and keep them. Mount them on paper with the date found.

4.   Check the dirty piece of paper for eggs (small, dark brown with a white mark sticking out at one end). Keep these carefully with the date found.

Measuring

1.   Every 7 days put the stick insect onto a piece of millimetre graph paper.

2.   Carefully put a pencil mark by each end of the stick insect. Return the stick insect to its jar. Measure the distance between the pencil marks. (Alternatively, or in addition, make a chart using strips of sticky paper equal to the insect's length.)

3.   Record any other observations in a diary.

2.   <u>Hens' Eggs</u>

        Kit: fertilized hens' eggs
                incubator
                candler (or box with a small light source)
                diaries

Preparation: See separate sheet

Watch the embryos developing using a candler. Weigh the eggs every day. Write down anything you notice happening in your diary. Watch the chicks developing after hatching. Write down anything you notice happening in a diary.

3.   <u>Height</u>

Make a graph of the heights of children in the class.

        (a)   Why do you think some children are taller than others?

        (b)   How long do you think you will stay this height?

        (c)   How tall do you think you will grow to be?

        (d)   What do you think makes you grow taller?

        (e)   Do people ever grow shorter?

4.   <u>Weight</u>

Make a graph of the weights of children in the class.

(a)   Why do you think some children are heavier than others?

(b)   How long do you think you will stay this weight?

(c)   How heavy do you think you will grow to be?

(d)   What do you think makes you grow heavier?

(e)   Do people ever grow lighter?

APPENDIX III

INDIVIDUAL INTERVIEWS (MARCH 1987)

These interviews use materials prepared in class activities. They may also be used with small groups.

1. Maize grown in a glass jar

    (a) What do you think is happening inside the seed?

    (b) Do you think the seed needs anything to make it grow?

    (c) What do you think maize plant needs to make it grow?

    (d) Do you think the seedling will go on growing in the jar if we keep on looking ater it?

    (e) What do you think the hairs on the root are for?

2. Carrot top

    Kit: sprouting carrot top in a saucer
          freshly cut, non-sprouting carrot top

Look at a carrot top which has sprouted in a saucer and compare it with a newly cut top.

    (a) What has happened to the carrot top?

    (b) Where do you think the leaves have come from?

    (c) Where do you think the roots have come from?

    (d) What do you think the carrot top needs to make it grow?

3. Bean sprouts

    Kit: mung beans
          bean sprouts

Look at some mung beans and some sprouts.

    (a)   List the similarities and differences between them.

    (b)   What is coming out of the seed?

    (c)   What do you think is happening inside the seeds?

    (d)   Do you think they can get any bigger?

    (e)   How could you make these seeds into sprouts?

4.   Runners

    Kit: plant with runners

Look at a plant with runners - spider plant, strawberry plant etc.

    (a)   What do you think is at the end of these stalks?

    (b)   Why do you think they are there?

    (c)   What do you think would happen if the stalk was cut?

    (d)   How do you think you could grow a baby spider plant?

Animals

1.   Stick Insects

    (a)   Do they need anything to make them grow?

(b)   Where do you think the new parts are coming from?

Watch them moulting.

(c)   What is happening to them?

(d)   What do you think the slit down the back is for?

(e)   Why do you think the stick insect splits?

(f)   Does anything like this happen to us or plants?

2.   <u>Hens' eggs</u>

(a)   Tell me what you think is happening inside the egg?

(b)   What do you think is making the 'chick' grow in the egg?

(c)   Do you think it will always stay inside the egg?

3.   <u>Chick</u>

(a)   What do you think the chick needs to make it grow?

(b)   Do you think it needs the same things as the egg did to make it grow?

(c)   How long do you think the chick will stay the size it is now?

(d)   Will the chick go on and on growing?

(e)   Where do the new bits of the chick come from?

APPENDIX IV

TEACHER PACK FOR EXPLORATION 2 (OCTOBER 1987)

ACTIVITIES

1. Potato

    Kit: potatoes

Leave potatoes which are developing eyes to sprout.

Preparation: Leave in the dark for at least 3 weeks.

Discussion

-   (a) What do you think has changed about the potato?

-   (b) Where do you think the shoots have come from?

-   (c) What do you think is happening inside the potato?

-   (d) What do you think it needs to help it grow?

-   (e) How do you think that helps it to grow?
        or What do you think makes it grow? How?

-   (f) Do you think the potato will go on growing like this?

-   (g) When do you think it grows?

2. Bean Sprouts

    Kit: mung beans
          large jam jar

Preparation: Soak the beans in a jar until the green casing begins to split (1 - 2 days). Pour off the water, rinse the seeds and drain them. Lay the jar on its side in a warm, dark place with the seeds spread out. Repeat the rinsing and draining until the sprouts are fully developed.

Discussion

-   (a) What has changed since you soaked the beans?

-   (b) Where do you think the leaves etc. have come from?

(c)　What do you think is happening inside the beans?

(d)　What do you think it needs to help it grow?

(e)　How do you think that helps it to grow?
or what do you think makes it grow?　How?

(f)　When do you think it grows?

(g)　Do you think it will go on growing?

3.　Broad Beans

Kit:　soil

transparent container (lemonade bottle)
broad beans

Preparation:　Plant at a depth of approximately 4-5 cms.

Discussion

(a)　What has happened to the bean since it was planted?

(b)　What do you think is happening inside the bean?

(c)　Do you think the bean needs anything to make it grow?

(d)　What do you think the broad bean plant needs to make it grow?

(e)　How do you think these things help it grow?
or What do you think makes it grow?　How?

(f)　When do you think it grows?

(g)　Do you think it will go on growing?

4.　Caterpillars and eggs

Incubation of eggs

Keep the eggs at a reasonably constant temperature, that is, out of sunlight and away from windows at night.　They should hatch in 7-10 days.

After about 5 days stand the eggs and their piece of cabbage leaf on a fresh cabbage leaf so that they have something on which to feed when they hatch.

During the course of incubation, the pigmentation of the eggs gradually changes from a very pale straw colour to a dark yellow. A few hours before hatching, the eggs turn black and the form of the caterpillar can be seen through the shell. [The eggs are small, so keep a x20 or x10 magnifier handy].

Hatching is not as spectacular as hens' eggs. The first caterpillars to hatch often start to eat the tops of the shells of the other larvae, ensuring that the entire batch of eggs hatch within about thirty minutes. They then eat the egg shells and spin a silk pad upon which to rest when they are not feeding.

Routine Maintenance

The caterpillar cage

A shoe box whose sides have been cut out and replaced by gauze should be adequate. Line the floor of the cage with several layers of newspaper, the top layer of which should be removed every day.

Feeding

The caterpillars feed on cabbage leaves (or nasturtium leaves if you run out). The cabbage you have been given has been organically grown so it has no insecticide on it which could kill the caterpillars off. The outer leaves of the cabbage are the best to use as food, and if these are removed regularly it will encourage the inner leaves to expand and form more large, outer leaves. Cabbage, unfortunately, becomes smelly rather quickly so it is important that the cage is cleaned and the cabbage changed every day.

Try not to handle the caterpillars when changing the cabbage. If you put fresh cabbage in next to the old, the caterpillars move themselves and the old cabbage can be removed later.

The caterpillars should remain as caterpillars for at least three weeks before pupating. During this time they moult four times. If the caterpillars are given less than 12 hours daylight a day, their pupation will be indefinite (they enter 'diapause'). This solves the potential problem of what should be done with any butterflies. It is best to cover the cage overnight to ensure both that the pupae enter diapause and that the temperature does not drop too low.

Any caterpillar which hangs limply from the cabbage should be removed before it infects the others.

Discussion

Eggs

(a)   What do you think is happening inside the egg?

(b)   What do you think the caterpillar needs to make it grow inside the egg?

(c)   How do you think these things help it to grow? What do you think makes the caterpillar grow inside the egg?

Caterpillars

(a)   What has happened to it?

(b)   Do you think it needs anything to help it grow?

(c)   How do you think that helps it go grow?
or What do you think makes it grow? How?

(d)   What do you think is happening inside it?

WORDS TO BE CLARIFIED IN INTERVIEW/DISCUSSION

Growth

Grown/grow

(e)   When do you think it grows?

(f)   Do you think it will go on growing?

Sunshine

EXPLORATORY TASKS

1. Activity - caterpillar eggs
   Timing - any time before hatching

   Draw a picture of/write about what you think is happening inside the eggs.

2. Activity - plant growth
   Timing - when beans are established

   Draw a picture of a plant in the place you would put it for it to grow very well. Show everything you think the plant would need.

3. Activity - animal growth
   Timing - when caterpillars approx. 4 - 5 days old
   Draw a picture of your caterpillar and what he is doing today. Next to it draw what you think he will be like tomorrow, and the day after... so you end up with five pictures. (or describe this in words)

QUESTIONS AND RESPONSE CHECK-LIST

These checklists are to help you build up an impression of the ideas which your children hold. There is room for you to add any comments you wish to make as well as ticks/tallymarks. You might like to look at each child individually or just get an impression of how common different ideas are in your class (this is probably more feasible).

The questions are meant to be used informally, as appropriate, not worked through from beginning to end. Additionally, the responses are there as a guide for you to check off against, rather than a source of "How many of you think it's the water?" They are not there for you to feed them in as ideas. You want to know your children's ideas so listen out for them telling you.

These check-lists will be a valuable source of information for you during the intervention period; it is worth keeping a note of the dates when you make any particularly relevant observations.

You will also find a sheet of words whose meanings need to be clarified. It's important to make sure what a child means when they say that something has disappeared, for example. The conventional meanings, and breadth of meaning, of words can't be assumed. Any further words which you feel should be on this list, please add them and share them at the meeting.

APPENDIX V

GROWTH

<u>Interview Questions (October 1987 - January 1988)</u>

Growth in water

(a)   What has happened since you first saw these beans?

(b)   Where do you think the leaves etc. have come from?

(c)   What do you think is happening/has happened inside the bean?

(d)   What do you think the bean needs to help it grow?

(e)   What do you think makes it grow and how?

   or   How do you think these things help it to grow?

(f)   When do you think it grows?

(g)   Do you think it will go on growing?

Growth in Soil

(a)   What has happened since the bean was planted?

(b)   Where do you think the leaves etc. have come from?

(c)   What do you think is happening/has happened inside the bean?

(d)   What do you think the plant needs to help it grow?

(e)   What do you think makes it grow and how?

   or   How do you think these things help it to grow?

(f)   When do you think the plant grows?

Potato

(a)   What has changed about the potato?

(b)   Where do you think the shoots have come from?

(c)   What do you think is happening inside the potato?

(g)   Do you think it will go on growing?

(d)   What do you think the potato needs in order to grow?

(e)   What makes it grow?

(f)   Do you think the potato will go on growing like this?

(g)   When do you think it grows?

Eggs

(a)   What do you think is happening inside the egg?

(b)   What do you think the caterpillar needs to make it grow inside the egg?

(c)   How do you think these things help it to grow? What do you think makes the caterpillars grow in eggs?

Animal growth

(a)   What has happened since you first saw the caterpillar? What has happened to you since you were measured last summer?

(b)   Does the caterpillar/do you need anything to help it/you grow?

(c)   How does that help it/you to grow?

      or   What makes it grow?

(d)   What do you think is happening inside the caterpillar/you to make you grow?

(e)   When do you think the caterpillar/you grows?

(f)   Do you think the caterpillar/you will go on growing?

APPENDIX VI

INTERVENTION STRATEGIES (NOVEMBER 1987)

INTERVENTION

Using children's ideas as the starting point for classroom activities

Aims

1. To work with the children's ideas, using them as a starting point for classroom activities.

2. To monitor and record your children's ideas.

3. To evaluate the different types of intervention which you try.

How you might go about it

1. Children have lots of ideas about a whole range of topic. Please don't tackle more than you feel you can manage. You might choose to

    (a) pick one area (e.g. metals, plant growth, evaporation/condensation) to explore with your class;
    (b) divide your class into groups with each group exploring a different area;
    (c) do something in between these.

Please hold a minimum of four sessions based upon this SPACE work which should incorporate at least three relevant activities from the ideas sheet. These will include one each of:

    1. Try out children's own ideas
    2. Vocabulary
    3. Generalisations

2. You have noted the ideas your class have already. It is important to see if and how these ideas develop through the intervention period. Pick at least one child for each intervention activity and look at how their ideas are influenced by the activity.

3. Your views on the success of the intervention activity are very important. Please evaluate briefly the different types of intervention which you try in terms both of their success in developing ideas and as class activities.

Support

We hope to visit every school once a week during the intervention. These visits are intended to help you, not to judge you. Please ring me up if you want to talk about anything.

Working Together to Safeguard Children

A guide to inter-agency working to safeguard and promote the welfare of children

To purchase a copy please visit:

www.TheNationalCurriculum.com

or scan this code to take you there:

© Crown copyright 2013
Corporate Author: The Department For Education
Published by: Shurville Publishing

This document is available online at www.education.gov.uk/aboutdfe/statutory

ISBN: 9780993064449

Contents

Summary

About this guidance

1. This guidance covers:

   - the legislative requirements and expectations on individual services to safeguard and promote the welfare of children; and

   - a clear framework for Local Safeguarding Children Boards (LSCBs) to monitor the effectiveness of local services.

2. This document replaces Working Together to Safeguard Children (2010); The Framework for the Assessment of Children in Need and their Families (2000); and Statutory guidance on making arrangements to safeguard and promote the welfare of children under section 11 of the Children Act 2004 (2007). Links to relevant supplementary guidance that professionals should consider alongside this guidance can be found at Appendix C.

What is the status of this guidance?

3. This guidance is issued under:

   - section 7 of the Local Authority Social Services Act 1970, which requires local authorities in their social services functions to act under the general guidance of the Secretary of State;

   - section 11(4) of the Children Act 2004 which requires each person or body to which the section 11 duty applies to have regard to any guidance given to them by the Secretary of State; and

   - section 16 of the Children Act 2004, which states that local authorities and each of the statutory partners must, in exercising their functions relating to Local Safeguarding Children Boards, have regard to any guidance given to them by the Secretary of State.

4. This guidance applies to other organisations as set out in chapter 2.

5. This guidance will come into effect from 15 April 2013.

Who is this guidance for?

6. Local authority Chief Executives and Directors of Children's Services are required to follow this statutory guidance, as they exercise their social services functions, unless exceptional reasons apply. It should be read and followed by LSCB Chairs and senior managers within organisations who commission and provide services for children and families, including social workers and professionals from health services, adult services, the police, Academy Trusts, education and the voluntary and community sector who have contact with children and families.[1,2]

7. All relevant professionals should read and comply with this guidance unless exceptional circumstances arise so that they can respond to individual children's needs appropriately.

---

[1] Department for Education *Statutory guidance on the roles and responsibilities of the Director of Children's Services and the Lead Member for Children's Services.*

[2] The reference to social workers throughout the documents means social workers who are registered to practice with the Health and Care Professions Council.

Introduction

1. Safeguarding children - the action we take to promote the welfare of children and protect them from harm - is everyone's responsibility. Everyone who comes into contact with children and families has a role to play.[3]

2. Safeguarding and promoting the welfare of children is defined for the purposes of this guidance as:

   - protecting children from maltreatment;

   - preventing impairment of children's health or development;

   - ensuring that children grow up in circumstances consistent with the provision of safe and effective care; and

   - taking action to enable all children to have the best outcomes.

3. In 2011-12 over 600,000 children in England were referred to local authority children's social care services by individuals who had concerns about their welfare.

4. For children who need additional help, every day matters. Academic research is consistent in underlining the damage to children from delaying intervention. The actions taken by professionals to meet the needs of these children as early as possible can be critical to their future.

5. Children are best protected when professionals are clear about what is required of them individually, and how they need to work together.

6. This guidance aims to help professionals understand what they need to do, and what they can expect of one another, to safeguard children. It focuses on core legal requirements and it makes clear what individuals and organisations should do to keep children safe. In doing so, it seeks to emphasise that effective safeguarding systems are those where:

   - the child's needs are paramount, and the needs and wishes of each child, be they a baby or infant, or an older child, should be put first, so that every child receives the support they need before a problem escalates;

   - all professionals who come into contact with children and families are alert to their needs and any risks of harm that individual abusers, or potential abusers, may pose to children;

   - all professionals share appropriate information in a timely way and can discuss any concerns about an individual child with colleagues and local authority children's social care;

---

[3] In this document a child is defined as anyone who has not yet reached their 18th birthday. 'Children' therefore means 'children and young people' throughout.

- high quality professionals are able to use their expert judgement to put the child's needs at the heart of the safeguarding system so that the right solution can be found for each individual child;

- all professionals contribute to whatever actions are needed to safeguard and promote a child's welfare and take part in regularly reviewing the outcomes for the child against specific plans and outcomes;

- LSCBs coordinate the work to safeguard children locally and monitor and challenge the effectiveness of local arrangements;

- when things go wrong Serious Case Reviews (SCRs) are published and transparent about any mistakes which were made so that lessons can be learnt; and

- local areas innovate and changes are informed by evidence and examination of the data.

7. Ultimately, effective safeguarding of children can only be achieved by putting children at the centre of the system, and by every individual and agency playing their full part, working together to meet the needs of our most vulnerable children.

A child-centred and coordinated approach to safeguarding

Key principles

8. Effective safeguarding arrangements in every local area should be underpinned by two key principles:

- safeguarding is everyone's responsibility: for services to be effective each professional and organisation should play their full part; and

- a child-centred approach: for services to be effective they should be based on a clear understanding of the needs and views of children.

Safeguarding is everyone's responsibility

9. Everyone who works with children - including teachers, GPs, nurses, midwives, health visitors, early years professionals, youth workers, police, Accident and Emergency staff, paediatricians, voluntary and community workers and social workers - has a responsibility for keeping them safe.

10. No single professional can have a full picture of a child's needs and circumstances and, if children and families are to receive the right help at the right time, everyone who comes into contact with them has a role to play in identifying concerns, sharing information and taking prompt action.

11. In order that organisations and practitioners collaborate effectively, it is vital that every individual working with children and families is aware of the role that they have to play and the role of other professionals. In addition, effective

safeguarding requires clear local arrangements for collaboration between professionals and agencies.

12. This statutory guidance sets out key roles for individual organisations and key elements of effective local arrangements for safeguarding. It is very important these arrangements are strongly led and promoted at a local level, specifically by:

- a strong lead from local authority members, and the commitment of chief officers in all agencies, in particular the Director of Children's Services and Lead Member for Children's Services in each local authority; and

- effective local coordination and challenge by the LSCBs in each area (see chapter 3).

A child-centred approach

13. Effective safeguarding systems are child centred. Failings in safeguarding systems are too often the result of losing sight of the needs and views of the children within them, or placing the interests of adults ahead of the needs of children.

14. Children are clear what they want from an effective safeguarding system and this is described in the box on page 10.

15. Children want to be respected, their views to be heard, to have stable relationships with professionals built on trust and for consistent support provided for their individual needs. This should guide the behaviour of professionals. Anyone working with children should see and speak to the child; listen to what they say; take their views seriously; and work with them collaboratively when deciding how to support their needs. A child-centred approach is supported by:

- the Children Act 1989 (as amended by section 53 of the Children Act 2004). This Act requires local authorities to give due regard to a child's wishes when determining what services to provide under section 17 of the Children Act 1989, and before making decisions about action to be taken to protect individual children under section 47 of the Children Act 1989. These duties complement requirements relating to the wishes and feelings of children who are, or may be, looked after (section 22(4) Children Act 1989), including those who are provided with accommodation under section 20 of the Children Act 1989 and children taken into police protection (section 46(3)(d) of that Act);

- the Equality Act 2010 which puts a responsibility on public authorities to have due regard to the need to eliminate discrimination and promote equality of opportunity. This applies to the process of identification of need and risk faced by the individual child and the process of assessment. No child or group of children must be treated any less favourably than others in being able to access effective services which meet their particular needs; and

- the United Nations Convention on the Rights of the Child (UNCRC). This is an international agreement that protects the rights of children and provides a child-centred framework for the development of services to children. The UK Government ratified the UNCRC in 1991 and, by doing so, recognises children's rights to expression and receiving information.

Children have said that they need

- **Vigilance: to have adults notice when things are troubling them**

- **Understanding and action: to understand what is happening; to be heard and understood; and to have that understanding acted upon**

- **Stability: to be able to develop an on-going stable relationship of trust with those helping them**

- **Respect: to be treated with the expectation that they are competent rather than not**

- **Information and engagement: to be informed about and involved in procedures, decisions, concerns and plans**

- **Explanation: to be informed of the outcome of assessments and decisions and reasons when their views have not met with a positive response**

- **Support: to be provided with support in their own right as well as a member of their family**

- **Advocacy: to be provided with advocacy to assist them in putting forward their views**

16. In addition to individual practitioners shaping support around the needs of individual children, local agencies need to have a clear understanding of the collective needs of children locally when commissioning effective services. As part of that process, the Director of Public Health should ensure that the needs of vulnerable children are a key part of the Joint Strategic Needs Assessment that is developed by the health and wellbeing board.

Chapter 1: Assessing need and providing help

Early help

1. Providing early help is more effective in promoting the welfare of children than reacting later. Early help means providing support as soon as a problem emerges, at any point in a child's life, from the foundation years through to the teenage years.

2. Effective early help relies upon local agencies working together to:

   - identify children and families who would benefit from early help;

   - undertake an assessment of the need for early help; and

   - provide targeted early help services to address the assessed needs of a child and their family which focuses on activity to significantly improve the outcomes for the child. Local authorities, under section 10 of the Children Act 2004, have a responsibility to promote inter-agency cooperation to improve the welfare of children.

> ### Section 10
>
> Section 10 of the Children Act 2004 requires each local authority to make arrangements to promote cooperation between the authority, each of the authority's relevant partners and such other persons or bodies working with children in the local authority's area as the authority considers appropriate. The arrangements are to be made with a view to improving the wellbeing of all children in the authority's area, which includes protection from harm and neglect. The local authority's relevant partners are listed in Table A in Appendix B.

Identifying children and families who would benefit from early help

3. Local agencies should have in place effective ways to identify emerging problems and potential unmet needs for individual children and families. This requires all professionals, including those in universal services and those providing services to adults with children, to understand their role in identifying emerging problems and to share information with other professionals to support early identification and assessment.

4. Local Safeguarding Children Boards (LSCBs) should monitor and evaluate the effectiveness of training, including multi-agency training, for all professionals in the area. Training should cover how to identify and respond early to the needs

of all vulnerable children, including: unborn children; babies; older children; young carers; disabled children; and those who are in secure settings.

5. Professionals should, in particular, be alert to the potential need for early help for a child who:

   - is disabled and has specific additional needs;
   - has special educational needs;
   - is a young carer;
   - is showing signs of engaging in anti-social or criminal behaviour;
   - is in a family circumstance presenting challenges for the child, such as substance abuse, adult mental health, domestic violence; and/or
   - is showing early signs of abuse and/or neglect.

6. Professionals working in universal services have a responsibility to identify the symptoms and triggers of abuse and neglect, to share that information and work together to provide children and young people with the help they need. Practitioners need to continue to develop their knowledge and skills in this area. They should have access to training to identify and respond early to abuse and neglect, and to the latest research showing what types of interventions are the most effective.

Effective assessment of the need for early help

7. Local agencies should work together to put processes in place for the effective assessment of the needs of individual children who may benefit from early help services.

8. Children and families may need support from a wide range of local agencies. Where a child and family would benefit from coordinated support from more than one agency (e.g. education, health, housing, police) there should be an inter-agency assessment. These early help assessments, such as the use of the Common Assessment Framework (CAF), should identify what help the child and family require to prevent needs escalating to a point where intervention would be needed via a statutory assessment under the Children Act 1989 (paragraph 26).

9. The early help assessment should be undertaken by a lead professional who should provide support to the child and family, act as an advocate on their behalf and coordinate the delivery of support services. The lead professional role could be undertaken by a General Practitioner (GP), family support worker, teacher, health visitor and/or special educational needs coordinator. Decisions about who should be the lead professional should be taken on a case by case basis and should be informed by the child and their family.

10. For an early help assessment to be effective:

   - the assessment should be undertaken with the agreement of the child and their parents or carers. It should involve the child and family as well as all the professionals who are working with them;

   - a teacher, GP, health visitor, early years' worker or other professional should be able to discuss concerns they may have about a child and family with a social worker in the local authority. Local authority children's social care should set out the process for how this will happen; and

   - if parents and/or the child do not consent to an early help assessment, then the lead professional should make a judgement as to whether, without help, the needs of the child will escalate. If so, a referral into local authority children's social care may be necessary.

11. If at any time it is considered that the child may be a child in need as defined in the Children Act 1989, or that the child has suffered significant harm or is likely to do so, a referral should be made immediately to local authority children's social care. This referral can be made by any professional.

Provision of effective early help services

12. The early help assessment carried out for an individual child and their family should be clear about the action to be taken and services to be provided (including any relevant timescales for the assessment) and aim to ensure that early help services are coordinated and not delivered in a piecemeal way.

13. Local areas should have a range of effective, evidence-based services in place to address assessed needs early. The early help on offer should draw upon the local assessment of need and the latest evidence of the effectiveness of early help and early intervention programmes. In addition to high quality support in universal services, specific local early help services will typically include family and parenting programmes, assistance with health issues and help for problems relating to drugs, alcohol and domestic violence. Services may also focus on improving family functioning and building the family's own capability to solve problems; this should be done within a structured, evidence-based framework involving regular review to ensure that real progress is being made. Some of these services may be delivered to parents but should always be evaluated to demonstrate the impact they are having on the outcomes for the child.

Accessing help and services

14. The provision of early help services should form part of a continuum of help and support to respond to the different levels of need of individual children and families.

15. Where need is relatively low level individual services and universal services may be able to take swift action. For other emerging needs a range of early help services may be required, coordinated through an early help assessment, as set out above. Where there are more complex needs, help may be provided under section 17 of the Children Act 1989 (children in need). Where there are child protection concerns (reasonable cause to suspect a child is suffering or likely to suffer significant harm) local authority social care services must make enquiries and decide if any action must be taken under section 47 of the Children Act 1989.

16. It is important that there are clear criteria for taking action and providing help across this full continuum. Having clear thresholds for action which are understood by all professionals, and applied consistently, should ensure that services are commissioned effectively and that the right help is given to the child at the right time.

17. The LSCB should agree with the local authority and its partners the levels for the different types of assessment and services to be commissioned and delivered. Local authority children's social care has the responsibility for clarifying the process for referrals.

18. The LSCB should publish a **threshold document** that includes:

   - the process for the early help assessment and the type and level of early help services to be provided; and

   - the criteria, including the level of need, for when a case should be referred to local authority children's social care for assessment and for statutory services under:

     - section 17 of the Children Act 1989 (children in need);

     - section 47 of the Children Act 1989 (reasonable cause to suspect children suffering or likely to suffer significant harm);

     - section 31 (care orders); and

     - section 20 (duty to accommodate a child) of the Children Act 1989.

19. Anyone who has concerns about a child's welfare should make a referral to local authority children's social care. For example, referrals may come from: children themselves, teachers, a GP, the police, health visitors, family members and members of the public. Within local authorities, children's social care should act as the principal point of contact for welfare concerns relating to

children. Therefore, as well as clear protocols for professionals working with children, contact details should be signposted clearly so that children, parents and other family members are aware of who they can contact if they require advice and/or support.

20. When professionals refer a child, they should include any information they have on the child's developmental needs and the capacity of the child's parents or carers to meet those needs. This information may be included in any assessment, including the early help assessment, which may have been carried out prior to a referral into local authority children's social care. Where an early help assessment has already been undertaken it should be used to support a referral to local authority children's social care, however, this is not a prerequisite for making a referral.

21. Feedback should be given by local authority children's social care to the referrer on the decisions taken. Where appropriate, this feedback should include the reasons why a case may not meet the statutory threshold to be considered by local authority children's social care for assessment and suggestions for other sources of more suitable support.

Information sharing

22. Effective sharing of information between professionals and local agencies is essential for effective identification, assessment and service provision.

23. Early sharing of information is the key to providing effective early help where there are emerging problems. At the other end of the continuum, sharing information can be essential to put in place effective child protection services. Serious Case Reviews (SCRs) have shown how poor information sharing has contributed to the deaths or serious injuries of children.

24. Fears about sharing information cannot be allowed to stand in the way of the need to promote the welfare and protect the safety of children. To ensure effective safeguarding arrangements:

    ▪ all organisations should have arrangements in place which set out clearly the processes and the principles for sharing information between each other, with other professionals and with the LSCB; and

    ▪ no professional should assume that someone else will pass on information which they think may be critical to keeping a child safe. If a professional has concerns about a child's welfare and believes they are suffering or likely to suffer harm, then they should share the information with local authority children's social care.

25. *Information Sharing: Guidance for practitioners and managers (2008)* supports frontline practitioners, working in child or adult services, who have to make

decisions about sharing personal information on a case by case basis.[4] The guidance can be used to supplement local guidance and encourage good practice in information sharing.

Assessments under the Children Act 1989

Statutory requirements

26. Under the Children Act 1989, local authorities are required to provide services for children in need for the purposes of safeguarding and promoting their welfare. Local Authorities undertake assessments of the needs of individual children to determine what services to provide and action to take. The full set of statutory assessments is set out in the box below.

---

[4] Department for Education guidance on information sharing.

Statutory assessments under the Children Act 1989

- A child in need is defined under the Children Act 1989 as a child who is unlikely to achieve or maintain a satisfactory level of health or development, or their health and development will be significantly impaired, without the provision of services; or a child who is disabled. In these cases, assessments by a social worker are carried out under **section 17** of the Children Act 1989. Children in need may be assessed under section 17 of the Children Act 1989, in relation to their special educational needs, disabilities, or as a carer, or because they have committed a crime. The process for assessment should also be used for children whose parents are in prison and for asylum seeking children. When assessing children in need and providing services, specialist assessments may be required and, where possible, should be coordinated so that the child and family experience a coherent process and a single plan of action.

- Concerns about maltreatment may be the reason for a referral to local authority children's social care or concerns may arise during the course of providing services to the child and family. In these circumstances, local authority children's social care must initiate enquiries to find out what is happening to the child and whether protective action is required. Local authorities, with the help of other organisations as appropriate, also have a duty to make enquiries under **section 47** of the Children Act 1989 if they have reasonable cause to suspect that a child is suffering, or is likely to suffer, significant harm, to enable them to decide whether they should take any action to safeguard and promote the child's welfare. There may be a need for immediate protection whilst the assessment is carried out.

- Some children in need may require accommodation because there is no one who has parental responsibility for them, because they are lost or abandoned or because the person who has been caring for them is prevented from providing them with suitable accommodation or care. Under **section 20** of the Children Act 1989, the local authority has a duty to accommodate such children in need in their area.

- Following an application under **section 31A**, where a child is the subject of a care order, the local authority, as a corporate parent, must assess the child's needs and draw up a care plan which sets out the services which will be provided to meet the child's identified needs.

The purpose of assessment

27. Whatever legislation the child is assessed under, the purpose of the assessment is always:

    - to gather important information about a child and family;

    - to analyse their needs and/or the nature and level of any risk and harm being suffered by the child;

    - to decide whether the child is a child in need (section 17) and/or is suffering or likely to suffer significant harm (section 47); and

    - to provide support to address those needs to improve the child's outcomes to make them safe.

28. Assessment should be a dynamic process, which analyses and responds to the changing nature and level of need and/or risk faced by the child. A good assessment will monitor and record the impact of any services delivered to the child and family and review the help being delivered. Whilst services may be delivered to a parent or carer, the assessment should be focused on the needs of the child and on the impact any services are having on the child.

29. Good assessments support professionals to understand whether a child has needs relating to their care or a disability and/or is suffering, or likely to suffer, significant harm. The specific needs of disabled children and young carers should be given sufficient recognition and priority in the assessment process. Further guidance can be accessed at *Safeguarding Disabled Children - Practice Guidance (2009)* and *Recognised, valued and supported: Next steps for the Carers Strategy (2010).*[5,6]

30. Practitioners should be rigorous in assessing and monitoring children at risk of neglect to ensure they are adequately safeguarded over time. They should act decisively to protect the child by initiating care proceedings where existing interventions are insufficient.

31. Where a child becomes looked after the assessment will be the baseline for work with the family. Any needs which have been identified should be addressed before decisions are made about the child's return home. An assessment by a social worker is required before the child returns home under the Care Planning, Placement and Case Review (England) Regulations 2010. This will provide evidence of whether the necessary improvements have been made to ensure the child's safety when they return home.

---

[5] Department for Education Safeguarding Disabled Children - Practice Guidance (2009).

[6] Department for Health http://www.dh.gov.uk/en/Publicationsandstatistics/Publications/PublicationsPolicyAndGuidance/DH_12207 7.

The principles and parameters of a good assessment

32. High quality assessments:

   - are child centred. Where there is a conflict of interest, decisions should be made in the child's best interests;

   - are rooted in child development and informed by evidence;

   - are focused on action and outcomes for children;

   - are holistic in approach, addressing the child's needs within their family and wider community;

   - ensure equality of opportunity;

   - involve children and families;

   - build on strengths as well as identifying difficulties;

   - are integrated in approach;

   - are a continuing process not an event;

   - lead to action, including the provision and review of services; and

   - are transparent and open to challenge.

33. Research has shown that taking a systematic approach to enquiries using a conceptual model is the best way to deliver a comprehensive assessment for all children. A good assessment is one which investigates the following three domains, set out in the diagram on the next page:

   - the child's developmental needs, including whether they are suffering or likely to suffer significant harm;

   - parents' or carers' capacity to respond to those needs; and

   - the impact and influence of wider family, community and environmental circumstances.

34. The interaction of these domains requires careful investigation during the assessment. The aim is to reach a judgement about the nature and level of needs and/or risks that the child may be facing within their family. It is important that:

   - information is gathered and recorded systematically;

   - information is checked and discussed with the child and their parents/carers where appropriate;

   - differences in views about information are recorded; and

   - the impact of what is happening to the child is clearly identified.

Assessment Framework

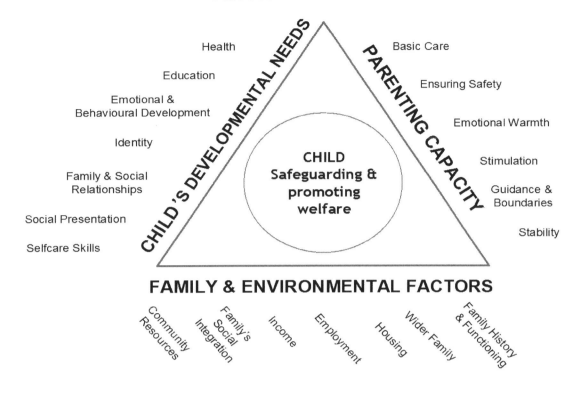

35. Assessments for some children - including young carers, children with special educational needs (who may require statements of SEN or Education Health and Care Plans subject to the passage of the Children and Families Bill), unborn children where there are concerns, asylum seeking children, children in hospital, disabled children, children with specific communication needs, children considered at risk of gang activity, children who are in the youth justice system - will require particular care.[7] Where a child has other assessments it is important that these are coordinated so that the child does not become lost between the different agencies involved and their different procedures.

Focusing on the needs and views of the child

36. Every assessment should be child centred. Where there is a conflict between the needs of the child and their parents/carers, decisions should be made in the child's best interests.

---

[7] Young carers are also entitled to request a separate carer's assessment under the Carers (Recognition and Services) Act 1995 and, if they are over 16 years, under the Carers and Disabled Children Act 2000.

37. Each child who has been referred into local authority children's social care should have an individual assessment to respond to their needs and to understand the impact of any parental behaviour on them as an individual. Local authorities have to give due regard to a child's age and understanding when determining what (if any) services to provide under section 17 of the Children Act 1989, and before making decisions about action to be taken to protect individual children under section 47 of the Children Act 1989.

38. Every assessment must be informed by the views of the child as well as the family. Children should, wherever possible, be seen alone and local authority children's social care has a duty to ascertain the child's wishes and feelings regarding the provision of services to be delivered.[8] It is important to understand the resilience of the individual child when planning appropriate services.

39. Every assessment should reflect the unique characteristics of the child within their family and community context. The Children Act 1989 promotes the view that all children and their parents should be considered as individuals and that family structures, culture, religion, ethnic origins and other characteristics should be respected.

40. Every assessment should draw together relevant information gathered from the child and their family and from relevant professionals including teachers, early years workers, health professionals, the police and adult social care.

41. A high quality assessment is one in which evidence is built and revised throughout the process. A social worker may arrive at a judgement early in the case but this may need to be revised as the case progresses and further information comes to light. It is a characteristic of skilled practice that social workers revisit their assumptions in the light of new evidence and take action to revise their decisions in the best interests of the individual child.

42. The aim is to use all the information to identify difficulties and risk factors as well as developing a picture of strengths and protective factors.

Developing a clear analysis

43. The social worker should analyse all the information gathered from the enquiry stage of the assessment to decide the nature and level of the child's needs and the level of risk, if any, they may be facing. The social work manager should challenge the social worker's assumptions as part of this process. An informed decision should be taken on the nature of any action required and which services should be provided. Social workers, their managers and other professionals should be mindful of the requirement to understand the level of

---

[8] Section 17 and 47 of the Children Act 1989, amended by section 53 Children Act 2004.

need and risk in a family from the child's perspective and ensure action or commission services which will have maximum impact on the child's life.

44. No system can fully eliminate risk. Understanding risk involves judgement and balance. To manage risks, social workers and other professionals should make decisions with the best interests of the child in mind, informed by the evidence available and underpinned by knowledge of child development.

45. Critical reflection through supervision should strengthen the analysis in each assessment.

46. Social workers, their managers and other professionals should always consider the plan from the child's perspective. A desire to think the best of adults and to hope they can overcome their difficulties should not trump the need to rescue children from chaotic, neglectful and abusive homes. Social workers and managers should always reflect the latest research on the impact of neglect and abuse when analysing the level of need and risk faced by the child. This should be reflected in the case recording.

47. Assessment is a dynamic and continuous process which should build upon the history of every individual case, responding to the impact of any previous services and analysing what further action might be needed. Social workers should build on this with help from other professionals from the moment that a need is identified.

48. Decision points and review points involving the child and family and relevant professionals should be used to keep the assessment on track. This is to ensure that help is given in a timely and appropriate way and that the impact of this help is analysed and evaluated in terms of the improved outcomes and welfare of the child.

Focusing on outcomes

49. Every assessment should be focused on outcomes, deciding which services and support to provide to deliver improved welfare for the child.

50. Where the outcome of the assessment is continued local authority children's social care involvement, the social worker and their manager should agree a plan of action with other professionals and discuss this with the child and their family. The plan should set out what services are to be delivered, and what actions are to be undertaken, by whom and for what purpose.

51. Many services provided will be for parents or carers. The plan should reflect this and set clear measurable outcomes for the child and expectations for the parents, with measurable, reviewable actions for them.

52. The plan should be reviewed regularly to analyse whether sufficient progress has been made to meet the child's needs and on the level of risk faced by the

child. This will be important for neglect cases where parents and carers can make small improvements. The test should be whether any improvements in adult behaviour are sufficient and sustained. Social workers and their managers should consider the need for further action and record their decisions. The review points should be agreed by the social worker with other professionals and with the child and family to continue evaluating the impact of any change on the welfare of the child.

53. Effective professional supervision can play a critical role in ensuring a clear focus on a child's welfare. Supervision should support professionals to reflect critically on the impact of their decisions on the child and their family. The social worker and their manager should review the plan for the child. Together they should ask whether the help given is leading to a significant positive change for the child and whether the pace of that change is appropriate for the child. Any professional working with vulnerable children should always have access to a manager to talk through their concerns and judgements affecting the welfare of the child. Assessment should remain an ongoing process, with the impact of services informing future decisions around action.

Timeliness

54. The timeliness of an assessment is a critical element of the quality of that assessment and the outcomes for the child. The speed with which an assessment is carried out after a child's case has been referred into local authority children's social care should be determined by the needs of the individual child and the nature and level of any risk of harm faced by the child. This will require judgements to be made by the social worker in discussion with their manager on each individual case.

55. Within **one working day** of a referral being received, a local authority social worker should make a decision about the type of response that is required and acknowledge receipt to the referrer.

56. For children who are in need of immediate protection, action must be taken by the social worker, or the police or NSPCC if removal is required, as soon as possible after the referral has been made to local authority children's social care (sections 44 and 46 of the Children Act 1989).

57. The maximum timeframe for the assessment to conclude, such that it is possible to reach a decision on next steps, should be no longer than 45 working days from the point of referral. If, in discussion with a child and their family and other professionals, an assessment exceeds 45 working days the social worker should record the reasons for exceeding the time limit.

58. Whatever the timescale for assessment, where particular needs are identified at any stage of the assessment, social workers should not wait until the

assessment reaches a conclusion before commissioning services to support the child and their family. In some cases the needs of the child will mean that a quick assessment will be required.

59. The assessment of neglect cases can be difficult. Neglect can fluctuate both in level and duration. A child's welfare can, for example, improve following input from services or a change in circumstances and review, but then deteriorate once support is removed. Professionals should be wary of being too optimistic. Timely and decisive action is critical to ensure that children are not left in neglectful homes.

60. It is the responsibility of the social worker to make clear to children and families how the assessment will be carried out and when they can expect a decision on next steps.

61. To facilitate the shift to an assessment process which brings continuity and consistency for children and families, there will no longer be a requirement to conduct separate initial and core assessments. Local authorities should determine their local assessment processes through a local protocol.

Local protocols for assessment

62. Local authorities, with their partners, should develop and publish local protocols for assessment. A local protocol should set out clear arrangements for how cases will be managed once a child is referred into local authority children's social care and be consistent with the requirements of this statutory guidance. The detail of each protocol will be led by the local authority in discussion with their partners and agreed with the relevant LSCB.

63. The local authority is publicly accountable for this protocol and all organisations and agencies have a responsibility to understand their local protocol.

The local protocol for assessment should:

- ensure that assessments are timely, transparent and proportionate to the needs of individual children and their families;

- set out how the needs of disabled children, young carers and children involved in the youth justice system will be addressed in the assessment process;

- clarify how agencies and professionals undertaking assessments and providing services can make contributions;

- clarify how the statutory assessments will be informed by other specialist assessments, such as the assessment for children with special educational needs (Education, Health and Care Plan) and disabled children;

- ensure that any specialist assessments are coordinated so that the child and family experience a joined up assessment process and a single planning process focused on outcomes;

- set out how shared internal review points with other professionals and the child and family will be managed throughout the assessment process;

- set out the process for assessment for children who are returned from care to live with their families;

- seek to ensure that each child and family understands the type of help offered and their own responsibilities, so as to improve the child's outcomes;

- set out the process for challenge by children and families by publishing the complaints procedures; and

- require decisions to be recorded in accordance with locally agreed procedures. Recording should include information on the child's development so that progress can be monitored to ensure their outcomes are improving. This will reduce the need for repeat assessments during care proceedings, which can be a major source of delay.

Processes for managing individual cases

64. The following descriptors and flow charts set out the precise steps that professionals should take when working together to assess and provide services for children who may be in need, including those suffering harm. The flow charts cover:

- the referral process into local authority children's social care;

- the process for determining next steps for a child who has been assessed as being 'in need'; and

- the essential processes for children where there is reasonable cause to suspect that the child is suffering, or likely to suffer, significant harm (this includes immediate protection for children at serious risk of harm).

Response to a referral

Once the referral has been accepted by local authority children's social care the lead professional role falls to a social worker.

The social worker should clarify with the referrer, when known, the nature of the concerns and how and why they have arisen.

Within **one working day** of a referral being received a local authority social worker should **make a decision** about the type of response that is required. This will include determining whether:

- the child requires immediate protection and urgent action is required;
- the child is in need, and should be assessed under section 17 of the Children Act 1989;
- there is reasonable cause to suspect that the child is suffering, or likely to suffer, significant harm, and whether enquires must be made and the child assessed under section 47 of the Children Act 1989;
- any services are required by the child and family and what type of services; and
- further specialist assessments are required in order to help the local authority to decide what further action to take.

Action to be taken:

The child and family must be informed of the action to be taken.

Local authority children's social care should see the child as soon as possible if the decision is taken that the referral requires further assessment.

Where requested to do so by local authority children's social care, professionals from other parts of the local authority such as housing and those in health organisations have a duty to cooperate under section 27 of the Children Act 1989 by assisting the local authority in carrying out its children's social care functions. This duty also applies to other local authorities.

Flow chart 1: Action taken when a child is referred to local authority children's social care services

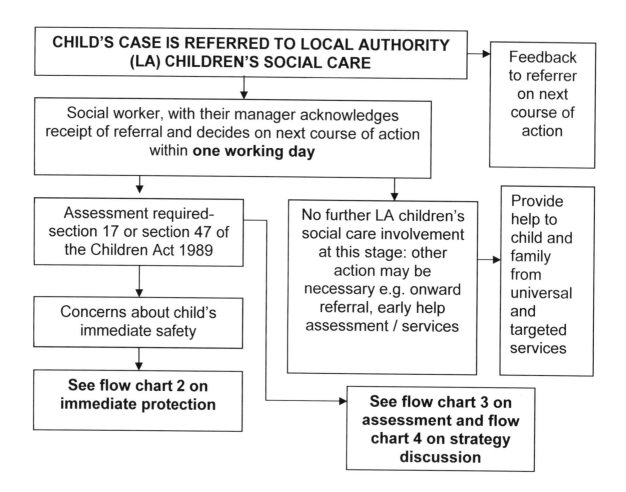

CHILD'S CASE IS REFERRED TO LOCAL AUTHORITY (LA) CHILDREN'S SOCIAL CARE

Feedback to referrer on next course of action

Social worker, with their manager acknowledges receipt of referral and decides on next course of action within **one working day**

Assessment required- section 17 or section 47 of the Children Act 1989

No further LA children's social care involvement at this stage: other action may be necessary e.g. onward referral, early help assessment / services

Provide help to child and family from universal and targeted services

Concerns about child's immediate safety

See flow chart 2 on immediate protection

See flow chart 3 on assessment and flow chart 4 on strategy discussion

Immediate Protection

Where there is a risk to the life of a child or a likelihood of serious immediate harm, local authority social workers, the police or NSPCC must use their statutory child protection powers to **act immediately to secure the safety of the child**.

If it is necessary to remove a child from their home, a local authority must, wherever possible and unless a child's safety is otherwise at immediate risk, apply for an **Emergency Protection Order (EPO)**. Police powers to remove a child in an emergency should be used only in exceptional circumstances where there is insufficient time to seek an EPO or for reasons relating to the immediate safety of the child.

An **EPO,** made by the court, gives authority to remove a child and places them under the protection of the applicant.

When considering whether emergency action is necessary an agency should always consider the needs of other children in the same household or in the household of an alleged perpetrator.

The local authority in whose area a child is found in circumstances that require emergency action (the first authority) is responsible for taking emergency action.

If the child is looked after by, or the subject of a child protection plan in another authority, the first authority must consult the authority responsible for the child. Only when the second local authority explicitly accepts responsibility (to be followed up in writing) is the first authority relieved of its responsibility to take emergency action.

Multi-agency working

Planned emergency action will normally take place following an immediate strategy discussion. Social workers, the police or NSPCC should:

- initiate a strategy discussion to discuss planned emergency action. Where a single agency has to act immediately, a strategy discussion should take place as soon as possible after action has been taken;

- see the child (this should be done by a practitioner from the agency taking the emergency action) to decide how best to protect them and whether to seek an EPO; and

- wherever possible, obtain legal advice before initiating legal action, in particular when an EPO is being sought.

Related information: *For further guidance on EPOs see pages 55-65 of Volume 1 of the Children Act Guidance and Regulations, Court Orders.*

Flow chart 2: Immediate protection

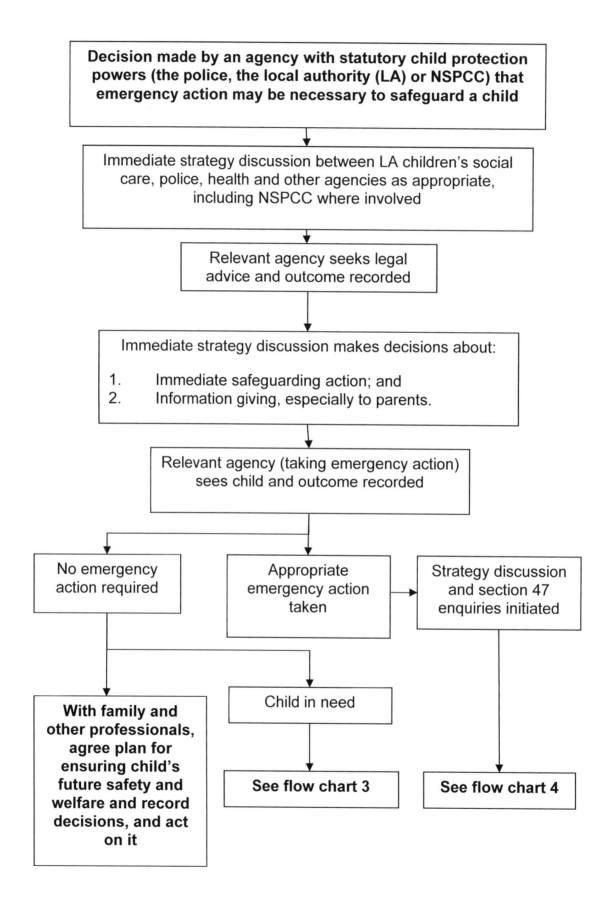

Decision made by an agency with statutory child protection powers (the police, the local authority (LA) or NSPCC) that emergency action may be necessary to safeguard a child

↓

Immediate strategy discussion between LA children's social care, police, health and other agencies as appropriate, including NSPCC where involved

↓

Relevant agency seeks legal advice and outcome recorded

↓

Immediate strategy discussion makes decisions about:

1.   Immediate safeguarding action; and
2.   Information giving, especially to parents.

↓

Relevant agency (taking emergency action) sees child and outcome recorded

No emergency action required

Appropriate emergency action taken

Strategy discussion and section 47 enquiries initiated

With family and other professionals, agree plan for ensuring child's future safety and welfare and record decisions, and act on it

Child in need

See flow chart 3

See flow chart 4

Assessment of a child under the Children Act 1989

Following acceptance of a referral by the local authority children's social care, a social worker should lead a multi-agency assessment under section 17 of the Children Act 1989. Local authorities have a duty to ascertain the child's wishes and feelings and take account of them when planning the provision of services. Assessments should be carried out in a timely manner reflecting the needs of the individual child, as set out in this chapter.

Where the local authority children's social care decides to provide services, a multi-agency child in need plan should be developed which sets out which agencies will provide which services to the child and family. The plan should set clear measurable outcomes for the child and expectations for the parents. The plan should reflect the positive aspects of the family situation as well as the weaknesses.

Where information gathered during an assessment (which may be very brief) results in the social worker suspecting that the child is suffering or likely to suffer significant harm, the local authority should hold a strategy discussion to enable it to decide, with other agencies, whether to initiate enquiries under section 47 of the Children Act 1989.

Purpose:	Assessments should determine whether the child is in need, the nature of any services required and whether any specialist assessments should be undertaken to assist the local authority in its decision making.
Social workers should:	<ul><li>lead on an assessment and complete it in line with the locally agreed protocol according to the child's needs and within **45 working days** from the point of referral into local authority children's social care;</li><li>see the child within a timescale that is appropriate to the nature of the concerns expressed at referral, according to an agreed plan;</li><li>conduct interviews with the child and family members, separately and together as appropriate. Initial discussions with the child should be conducted in a way that minimises distress to them and maximises the likelihood that they will provide accurate and complete information, avoiding leading or suggestive questions;</li><li>record the assessment findings and decisions and next steps following the assessment;</li><li>inform, in writing, all the relevant agencies and the family of their decisions and, if the child is a child in need, of the plan for providing support; and</li></ul>

	▪ inform the referrer of what action has been or will be taken.
The police should:	▪ assist other agencies to carry out their responsibilities where there are concerns about the child's welfare, whether or not a crime has been committed. If a crime has been committed, the police should be informed by the local authority children's social care.
All involved professionals should:	▪ be involved in the assessment and provide further information about the child and family; and ▪ agree further action including what services would help the child and family and inform local authority children's social care if any immediate action is required.

Flow chart 3: Action taken for an assessment of a child under the Children Act 1989.

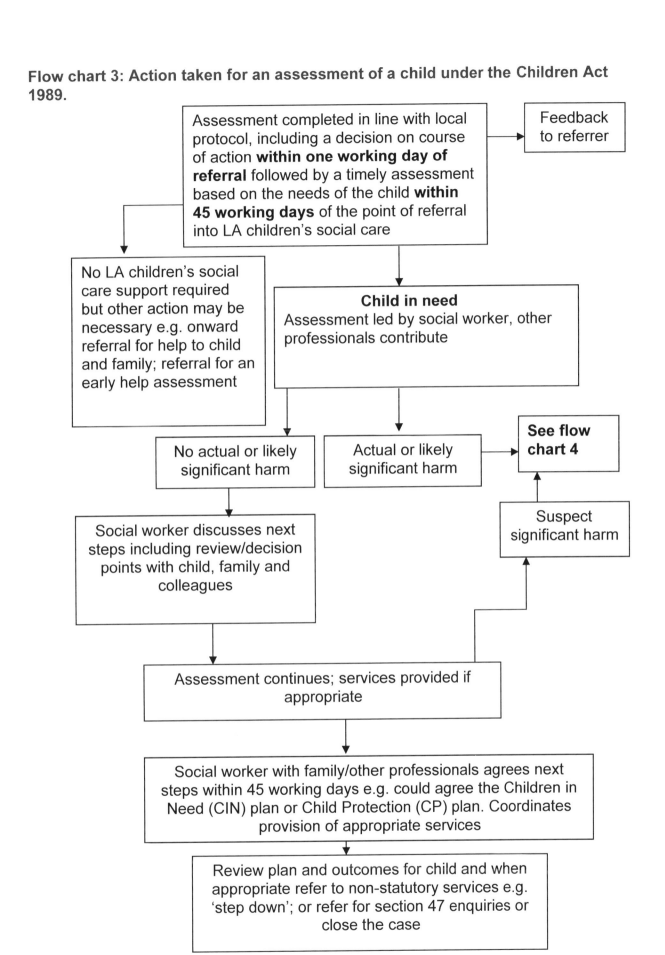

Assessment completed in line with local protocol, including a decision on course of action **within one working day of referral** followed by a timely assessment based on the needs of the child **within 45 working days** of the point of referral into LA children's social care

Feedback to referrer

No LA children's social care support required but other action may be necessary e.g. onward referral for help to child and family; referral for an early help assessment

Child in need
Assessment led by social worker, other professionals contribute

No actual or likely significant harm

Actual or likely significant harm

See flow chart 4

Suspect significant harm

Social worker discusses next steps including review/decision points with child, family and colleagues

Assessment continues; services provided if appropriate

Social worker with family/other professionals agrees next steps within 45 working days e.g. could agree the Children in Need (CIN) plan or Child Protection (CP) plan. Coordinates provision of appropriate services

Review plan and outcomes for child and when appropriate refer to non-statutory services e.g. 'step down'; or refer for section 47 enquiries or close the case

Strategy discussion

Whenever there is reasonable cause to suspect that a child is suffering, or is likely to suffer, significant harm there should be a strategy discussion involving local authority children's social care, the police, health and other bodies such as the referring agency. This might take the form of a multi-agency meeting or phone calls and more than one discussion may be necessary. A strategy discussion can take place following a referral or at any other time, including during the assessment process.

Purpose:	Local authority children's social care should convene a strategy discussion to determine the child's welfare and plan rapid future action if there is reasonable cause to suspect the child is suffering, or is likely to suffer, significant harm.
Strategy discussion attendees:	A local authority social worker and their manager, health professionals and a police representative should, as a minimum, be involved in the strategy discussion. Other relevant professionals will depend on the nature of the individual case but may include: • the professional or agency which made the referral; • the child's school or nursery; and • any health services the child or family members are receiving. All attendees should be sufficiently senior to make decisions on behalf of their agencies.
Strategy discussion tasks:	The discussion should be used to: • share available information; • agree the conduct and timing of any criminal investigation; and • decide whether enquiries under section 47 of the Children Act 1989 should be undertaken. Where there are grounds to initiate a section 47 of the Children Act 1989 enquiry, decisions should be made as to: • what further information is needed if an assessment is already underway and how it will be obtained and recorded; • what immediate and short term action is required to support the child, and who will do what by when; and • whether legal action is required. The timescale for the assessment to reach a decision on next steps should

	be based upon the needs of the individual child, consistent with the local protocol and certainly no longer than **45 working days** from the point of referral into local authority children's social care.

The principles and parameters for the assessment of children in need at chapter 1 paragraph 32 should be followed for assessments undertaken under section 47 of the Children Act 1989. |
| **Social workers with their managers should:** | <ul><li>convene the strategy discussion and make sure it:</li><li>considers the child's welfare and safety, and identifies the level of risk faced by the child;</li><li>decides what information should be shared with the child and family (on the basis that information is not shared if this may jeopardise a police investigation or place the child at risk of significant harm);</li><li>agrees what further action is required, and who will do what by when, where an EPO is in place or the child is the subject of police powers of protection;</li><li>records agreed decisions in accordance with local recording procedures; and</li><li>follows up actions to make sure what was agreed gets done.</li></ul> |
| **The police should:** | <ul><li>discuss the basis for any criminal investigation and any relevant processes that other agencies might need to know about, including the timing and methods of evidence gathering; and</li><li>lead the criminal investigation (local authority children's social care have the lead for the section 47 enquires and assessment of the child's welfare) where joint enquiries take place.</li></ul> |

Flow chart 4: Action following a strategy discussion

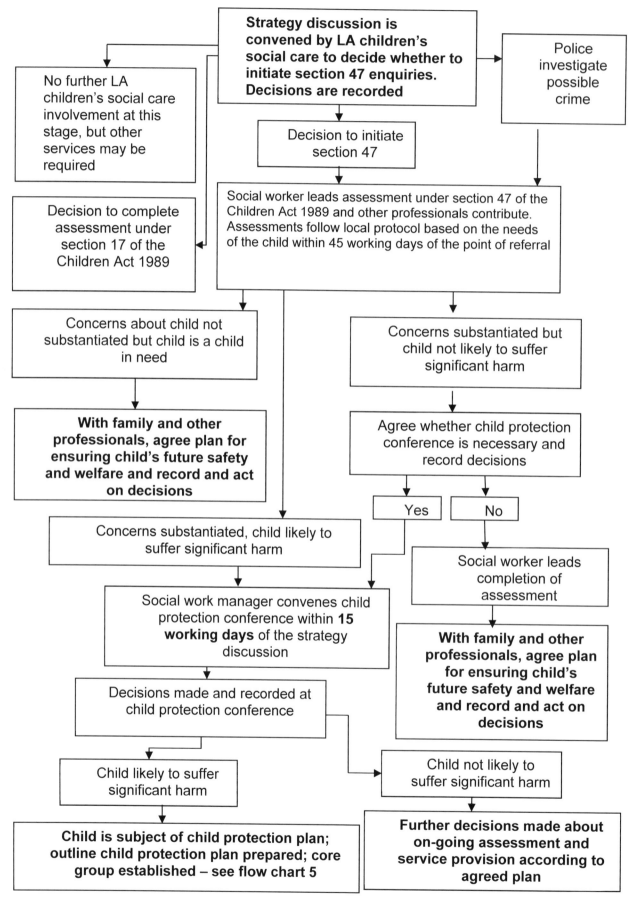

Strategy discussion is convened by LA children's social care to decide whether to initiate section 47 enquiries. Decisions are recorded

Police investigate possible crime

No further LA children's social care involvement at this stage, but other services may be required

Decision to initiate section 47

Decision to complete assessment under section 17 of the Children Act 1989

Social worker leads assessment under section 47 of the Children Act 1989 and other professionals contribute. Assessments follow local protocol based on the needs of the child within 45 working days of the point of referral

Concerns about child not substantiated but child is a child in need

Concerns substantiated but child not likely to suffer significant harm

With family and other professionals, agree plan for ensuring child's future safety and welfare and record and act on decisions

Agree whether child protection conference is necessary and record decisions

Yes

No

Concerns substantiated, child likely to suffer significant harm

Social worker leads completion of assessment

Social work manager convenes child protection conference within **15 working days** of the strategy discussion

With family and other professionals, agree plan for ensuring child's future safety and welfare and record and act on decisions

Decisions made and recorded at child protection conference

Child likely to suffer significant harm

Child not likely to suffer significant harm

Child is subject of child protection plan; outline child protection plan prepared; core group established – see flow chart 5

Further decisions made about on-going assessment and service provision according to agreed plan

Initiating section 47 enquiries

A section 47 enquiry is carried out by undertaking or continuing with an assessment in accordance with the guidance set out in this chapter and following the principles and parameters of a good assessment.

Local authority social workers have a statutory duty to lead assessments under section 47 of the Children Act 1989. The police, health professionals, teachers and other relevant professionals should help the local authority in undertaking its enquiries.

Purpose:	A section 47 enquiry is initiated to decide whether and what type of action is required to safeguard and promote the welfare of a child who is suspected of, or likely to be, suffering significant harm.
Social workers with their managers should:	<ul><li>lead the assessment in accordance with this guidance;</li><li>carry out enquiries in a way that minimises distress for the child and family;</li><li>see the child who is the subject of concern to ascertain their wishes and feelings; assess their understanding of their situation; assess their relationships and circumstances more broadly;</li><li>interview parents and/or caregivers and determine the wider social and environmental factors that might impact on them and their child;</li><li>systematically gather information about the child's and family's history;</li><li>analyse the findings of the assessment and evidence about what interventions are likely to be most effective with other relevant professionals to determine the child's needs and the level of risk of harm faced by the child to inform what help should be provided and act to provide that help; and</li><li>follow the guidance set out in *Achieving Best Evidence in Criminal Proceedings: Guidance on interviewing victims and witnesses, and guidance on using special measures*, where a decision has been made to undertake a joint interview of the child as part of any criminal investigation.[9]</li></ul>
The police should:	<ul><li>help other agencies understand the reasons for concerns about the child's safety and welfare;</li></ul>

---

[9] Ministry of Justice *Achieving Best Evidence in Criminal Proceedings: Guidance on interviewing victims and witnesses, and guidance on using special measures*.

	<ul><li>decide whether or not police investigations reveal grounds for instigating criminal proceedings;</li><li>make available to other professionals any evidence gathered to inform discussions about the child's welfare; and</li><li>follow the guidance set out in *Achieving Best Evidence in Criminal Proceedings: Guidance on interviewing victims and witnesses, and guidance on using special measures,* where a decision has been made to undertake a joint interview of the child as part of the criminal investigations.[10]</li></ul>
Health professionals should:	<ul><li>undertake appropriate medical tests, examinations or observations, to determine how the child's health or development may be being impaired;</li><li>provide any of a range of specialist assessments. For example, physiotherapists, occupational therapists, speech and language therapists and child psychologists may be involved in specific assessments relating to the child's developmental progress. The lead health practitioner (probably a consultant pediatrician, or possibly the child's GP) may need to request and coordinate these assessments; and</li><li>ensure appropriate treatment and follow up health concerns.</li></ul>
All involved professionals should:	<ul><li>contribute to the assessment as required, providing information about the child and family; and</li><li>consider whether a joint enquiry/investigation team may need to speak to a child victim without the knowledge of the parent or caregiver.</li></ul>

---

[10] Ministry of Justice *Achieving Best Evidence in Criminal Proceedings: Guidance on interviewing victims and witnesses, and guidance on using special measures*.

Outcome of section 47 enquiries

Local authority social workers are responsible for deciding what action to take and how to proceed following section 47 enquiries.

If local authority children's social care decides not to proceed with a child protection conference then other professionals involved with the child and family have the right to request that local authority children's social care convene a conference, if they have serious concerns that a child's welfare may not be adequately safeguarded. As a last resort, the LSCB should have in place a quick and straightforward means of resolving differences of opinion.

Where concerns of significant harm are not substantiated:	
Social workers with their managers should:	<ul><li>discuss the case with the child, parents and other professionals;</li><li>determine whether support from any services may be helpful and help secure it; and</li><li>consider whether the child's health and development should be re-assessed regularly against specific objectives and decide who has responsibility for doing this.</li></ul>
All involved professionals should:	<ul><li>participate in further discussions as necessary;</li><li>contribute to the development of any plan as appropriate;</li><li>provide services as specified in the plan for the child; and</li><li>review the impact of services delivered as agreed in the plan.</li></ul>

Where concerns of significant harm are substantiated and the child is judged to be suffering, or likely to suffer, significant harm:	
Social workers with their managers should:	<ul><li>convene an initial child protection conference (see next section for details). The timing of this conference should depend on the urgency of the case and respond to the needs of the child and the nature and severity of the harm they may be facing. The initial child protection conference should take place within **15 working days** of a strategy discussion, or the strategy discussion at which section 47 enquiries were initiated if more than one has been held;</li><li>consider whether any professionals with specialist knowledge should be invited to participate;</li><li>ensure that the child and their parents understand the purpose of the conference and who will attend; and</li><li>help prepare the child if he or she is attending or making representations through a third party to the conference. Give information about advocacy agencies and explain that the family may bring an advocate, friend or supporter.</li></ul>
All involved	<ul><li>contribute to the information their agency provides ahead of the conference, setting out the nature of the agency's</li></ul>

38

professionals should:	involvement with the child and family; <ul><li>consider, in conjunction with the police and the appointed conference Chair, whether the report can and should be shared with the parents and if so when; and</li><li>attend the conference and take part in decision making when invited.</li></ul>

Initial child protection conferences

Following section 47 enquiries, an initial child protection conference brings together family members (and the child where appropriate), with the supporters, advocates and professionals most involved with the child and family, to make decisions about the child's future safety, health and development. If concerns relate to an unborn child, consideration should be given as to whether to hold a child protection conference prior to the child's birth.

Purpose:	<ul><li>To bring together and analyse, in an inter-agency setting, all relevant information and plan how best to safeguard and promote the welfare of the child. It is the responsibility of the conference to make recommendations on how agencies work together to safeguard the child in future. Conference tasks include:</li><li>appointing a lead statutory body (either local authority children's social care or NSPCC) and a lead social worker, who should be a qualified, experienced social worker and an employee of the lead statutory body;</li><li>identifying membership of the core group of professionals and family members who will develop and implement the child protection plan;</li><li>establishing timescales for meetings of the core group, production of a child protection plan and for child protection review meetings; and</li><li>agreeing an outline child protection plan, with clear actions and timescales, including a clear sense of how much improvement is needed, by when, so that success can be judged clearly.</li></ul>
The Conference Chair:	<ul><li>is accountable to the Director of Children's Services. Where possible the same person should chair subsequent child protection reviews;</li><li>should be a professional, independent of operational and/or line management responsibilities for the case; and</li><li>should meet the child and parents in advance to ensure they understand the purpose and the process.</li></ul>
Social workers with their managers should:	<ul><li>convene, attend and present information about the reason for the conference, their understanding of the child's needs, parental capacity and family and environmental context and evidence of how the child has been abused or neglected and its impact on their health and development;</li><li>analyse the information to enable informed decisions about what action is necessary to safeguard and promote the welfare of the child who is the subject of the conference;</li><li>share the conference information with the child and family beforehand (where appropriate);</li><li>prepare a report for the conference on the child and family which sets out and analyses what is known about the child and family and the local authority's recommendation; and</li></ul>

	■ record conference decisions and recommendations and ensure action follows.
All involved professionals should:	■ work together to safeguard the child from harm in the future, taking timely, effective action according to the plan agreed.
LSCBs should:	■ monitor the effectiveness of these arrangements.

The child protection plan
Actions and responsibilities following the initial child protection conference

Purpose:	The aim of the child protection plan is to: <ul><li>ensure the child is safe from harm and prevent him or her from suffering further harm;</li><li>promote the child's health and development; and</li><li>support the family and wider family members to safeguard and promote the welfare of their child, provided it is in the best interests of the child.</li></ul>
Local authority children's social care should:	<ul><li>designate a social worker to be the lead professional as they carry statutory responsibility for the child's welfare;</li><li>consider the evidence and decide what legal action to take if any, where a child has suffered, or is likely to suffer, significant harm; and</li><li>define the local protocol for timeliness of circulating plans after the child protection conference.</li></ul>
Social workers with their managers should:	<ul><li>be the lead professional for inter-agency work with the child and family, coordinating the contribution of family members and professionals into putting the child protection plan into effect;</li><li>develop the outline child protection plan into a more detailed inter-agency plan and circulate to relevant professionals (and family where appropriate);</li><li>undertake direct work with the child and family in accordance with the child protection plan, taking into account the child's wishes and feelings and the views of the parents in so far as they are consistent with the child's welfare;</li><li>complete the child's and family's in-depth assessment, securing contributions from core group members and others as necessary;</li><li>explain the plan to the child in a manner which is in accordance with their age and understanding and agree the plan with the child;</li><li>coordinate reviews of progress against the planned outcomes set out in the plan, updating as required. The first review should be held within 3 months of the initial conference and further reviews at intervals of no more than 6 months for as long as the child remains subject of a child protection plan;</li><li>record decisions and actions agreed at core group meetings as well as the written views of those who were not able to attend, and follow up those actions to ensure they take place. The child protection plan should be updated as necessary; and</li><li>lead core group activity.</li></ul>

The core group should:	<ul><li>meet within 10 working days from the initial child protection conference if the child is the subject of a child protection plan;</li><li>develop the outline child protection plan, based on assessment findings, and set out what needs to change, by how much, and by when in order for the child to be safe and have their needs met;</li><li>decide what steps need to be taken, and by whom, to complete the in-depth assessment to inform decisions about the child's safety and welfare; and</li><li>implement the child protection plan and take joint responsibility for carrying out the agreed tasks, monitoring progress and outcomes, and refining the plan as needed.</li></ul>

Child protection review conference **The review conference procedures for preparation, decision-making and other procedures should be the same as those for an initial child protection conference.**	
Purpose:	To review whether the child is continuing to suffer, or is likely to suffer, significant harm, and review developmental progress against child protection plan outcomes. To consider whether the child protection plan should continue or should be changed.
Social workers with their managers should:	▪ attend and lead the organisation of the conference; ▪ determine when the review conference should be held within 3 months of the initial conference, and thereafter at maximum intervals of 6 months; ▪ provide information to enable informed decisions about what action is necessary to safeguard and promote the welfare of the child who is the subject of the child protection plan, and about the effectiveness and impact of action taken so far; ▪ share the conference information with the child and family beforehand, where appropriate; ▪ record conference outcomes; and ▪ decide whether to initiate family court proceedings (all the children in the household should be considered, even if concerns are only expressed about one child) if the child is considered to be suffering significant harm.
All involved professionals should:	▪ attend, when invited, and provide details of their involvement with the child and family; and ▪ produce reports for the child protection review. This information will provide an overview of work undertaken by family members and professionals, and evaluate the impact on the child's welfare against the planned outcomes set out in the child protection plan.

44

Flow chart 5: What happens after the child protection conference, including the review?

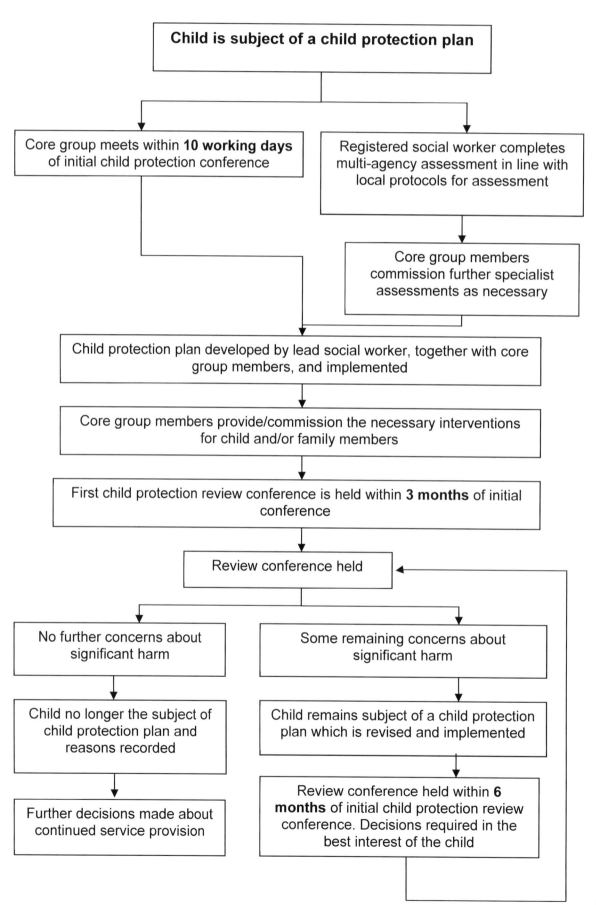

Child is subject of a child protection plan

Core group meets within **10 working days** of initial child protection conference

Registered social worker completes multi-agency assessment in line with local protocols for assessment

Core group members commission further specialist assessments as necessary

Child protection plan developed by lead social worker, together with core group members, and implemented

Core group members provide/commission the necessary interventions for child and/or family members

First child protection review conference is held within **3 months** of initial conference

Review conference held

No further concerns about significant harm

Some remaining concerns about significant harm

Child no longer the subject of child protection plan and reasons recorded

Child remains subject of a child protection plan which is revised and implemented

Further decisions made about continued service provision

Review conference held within **6 months** of initial child protection review conference. Decisions required in the best interest of the child

45

Discontinuing the Child Protection Plan	

A child should no longer be the subject of a child protection plan if:
 	
   ■ it is judged that the child is no longer continuing to, or is likely to, suffer significant harm and therefore no longer requires safeguarding by means of a child protection plan;
   ■ the child and family have moved permanently to another local authority area. In such cases, the receiving local authority should convene a child protection conference within 15 working days of being notified of the move. Only after this event may the original local authority discontinue its child protection plan; or
   ■ the child has reached 18 years of age (to end the child protection plan, the local authority should have a review around the child's birthday and this should be planned in advance), has died or has permanently left the United Kingdom.	

Social workers with their managers should:	■ notify, as a minimum, all agency representatives who were invited to attend the initial child protection conference that led to the plan; and ■ consider whether support services are still required and discuss with the child and family what might be needed, based on a re-assessment of the child's needs.

Chapter 2: Organisational responsibilities

1. The previous chapter set out the need for organisations, working together, to take a coordinated approach to ensure effective safeguarding arrangements. This is supported by the duty on local authorities under section 10 of the Children Act 2004 to make arrangements to promote cooperation to improve the wellbeing of all children in the authority's area.

2. In addition, a range of individual organisations and professionals working with children and families have specific statutory duties to promote the welfare of children and ensure they are protected from harm.

Section 11 of the Children Act 2004

Section 11 of the Children Act 2004 places duties on a range of organisations and individuals to ensure their functions, and any services that they contract out to others, are discharged having regard to the need to safeguard and promote the welfare of children.

Various other statutory duties apply to other specific organisations working with children and families and are set out in this chapter.

3. Section 11 places a duty on:

   - local authorities and district councils that provide children's and other types of services, including children's and adult social care services, public health, housing, sport, culture and leisure services, licensing authorities and youth services;

   - NHS organisations, including the NHS Commissioning Board and clinical commissioning groups, NHS Trusts and NHS Foundation Trusts;

   - the police, including police and crime commissioners and the chief officer of each police force in England and the Mayor's Office for Policing and Crime in London;

   - the British Transport Police;

   - the Probation Service;

   - Governors/Directors of Prisons and Young Offender Institutions;

   - Directors of Secure Training Centres; and

   - Youth Offending Teams/Services.

4. These organisations should have in place arrangements that reflect the importance of safeguarding and promoting the welfare of children, including:

   - a clear line of accountability for the commissioning and/or provision of services designed to safeguard and promote the welfare of children;

   - a senior board level lead to take leadership responsibility for the organisation's safeguarding arrangements;

- a culture of listening to children and taking account of their wishes and feelings, both in individual decisions and the development of services;

- arrangements which set out clearly the processes for sharing information, with other professionals and with the Local Safeguarding Children Board (LSCB);

- a designated professional lead (or, for health provider organisations, named professionals) for safeguarding. Their role is to support other professionals in their agencies to recognise the needs of children, including rescue from possible abuse or neglect. Designated professional roles should always be explicitly defined in job descriptions. Professionals should be given sufficient time, funding, supervision and support to fulfil their child welfare and safeguarding responsibilities effectively;

- safe recruitment practices for individuals whom the organisation will permit to work regularly with children, including policies on when to obtain a criminal record check;

- appropriate supervision and support for staff, including undertaking safeguarding training:

    - employers are responsible for ensuring that their staff are competent to carry out their responsibilities for safeguarding and promoting the welfare of children and creating an environment where staff feel able to raise concerns and feel supported in their safeguarding role;

    - staff should be given a mandatory induction, which includes familiarisation with child protection responsibilities and procedures to be followed if anyone has any concerns about a child's safety or welfare; and

    - all professionals should have regular reviews of their own practice to ensure they improve over time.

- clear policies in line with those from the LSCB for dealing with allegations against people who work with children. An allegation may relate to a person who works with children who has:

    - behaved in a way that has harmed a child, or may have harmed a child;

    - possibly committed a criminal offence against or related to a child; or

    - behaved towards a child or children in a way that indicates they may pose a risk of harm to children.

In addition:

- county level and unitary local authorities should have a Local Authority Designated Officer (LADO) to be involved in the management and oversight of individual cases. The LADO should provide advice and guidance to employers and voluntary organisations, liaising with the police and other agencies and monitoring the progress of cases to ensure that they are dealt with as quickly as possible, consistent with a thorough and fair process;

- any allegation should be reported immediately to a senior manager within the organisation. The LADO should also be informed within one working day of all allegations that come to an employer's attention or that are made directly to the police; and

- if an organisation removes an individual (paid worker or unpaid volunteer) from work such as looking after children (or would have, had the person not left first) because the person poses a risk of harm to children, the organisation must make a referral to the Disclosure and Barring Service. It is an offence to fail to make a referral without good reason.

Individual organisational responsibilities

5. In addition to these section 11 duties, which apply to a number of named organisations, further safeguarding duties are also placed on individual organisations through other statutes. The key duties that fall on each individual organisation are set out below.

Schools and colleges

6. Section 175 of the Education Act 2002 places a duty on local authorities (in relation to their education functions and governing bodies of maintained schools and further education institutions, which include sixth-form colleges) to exercise their functions with a view to safeguarding and promoting the welfare of children who are pupils at a school, or who are students under 18 years of age attending further education institutions. The same duty applies to independent schools (which include Academies and free schools) by virtue of regulations made under section 157 of the same Act.

7. In order to fulfil their duty under sections 157 and 175 of the Education Act 2002, all educational settings to whom the duty applies should have in place the arrangements set out in paragraph 4 of this chapter. In addition schools should have regard to specific guidance given by the Secretary of State under sections 157 and 175 of the Education Act 2002 namely, *Safeguarding Children and Safer Recruitment in Education and Dealing with allegations of abuse against teachers and other staff.*[11,12]

---

[11] DfE *Safeguarding Children and Safer Recruitment in Education.*
[12] DfE *Dealing with allegations of abuse against teachers and other staff.*

Early Years and Childcare

8. Early years providers have a duty under section 40 of the Childcare Act 2006 to comply with the welfare requirements of the Early Years Foundation Stage.[13] Early years providers should ensure that:

   - staff complete safeguarding training that enables them to recognise signs of potential abuse and neglect; and

   - they have a practitioner who is designated to take lead responsibility for safeguarding children within each early years setting and who should liaise with local statutory children's services agencies as appropriate. This lead should also complete child protection training.

Health Services

9. NHS organisations are subject to the section 11 duties set out in paragraph 4 of this chapter. Health professionals are in a strong position to identify welfare needs or safeguarding concerns regarding individual children and, where appropriate, provide support. This includes understanding risk factors, communicating effectively with children and families, liaising with other agencies, assessing needs and capacity, responding to those needs and contributing to multi-agency assessments and reviews.

10. A wide range of health professionals have a critical role to play in safeguarding and promoting the welfare of children including: GPs, primary care professionals, paediatricians, nurses, health visitors, midwives, school nurses, those working in maternity, child and adolescent mental health, adult mental health, alcohol and drug services, unscheduled and emergency care settings and secondary and tertiary care.

11. All staff working in healthcare settings - including those who predominantly treat adults - should receive training to ensure they attain the competences appropriate to their role and follow the relevant professional guidance. [14,15,16]

12. Within the NHS:[17]

   - the **NHS Commissioning Board** will be responsible for ensuring that the health commissioning system as a whole is working effectively to

---

[13] DfE guidance on the welfare requirements of the Early Years Foundation Stage.

[14] Safeguarding Children and Young People: roles and competences for health care staff, RCPCH (2010).

[15] Looked after children: Knowledge, skills and competences of health care staff, RCN and RCPCH, (2012).

[16] For example, Protecting children and young people: the responsibilities of all doctors, GMC (2012).

[17] Further guidance on accountabilities for safeguarding children in the NHS is available in the NHS Commissioning Board document http://www.commissioningboard.nhs.uk/wp-content/uploads/2013/03/safeguarding-vulnerable-people.pdf

safeguard and promote the welfare of children. It will also be accountable for the services it directly commissions. The NHS Commissioning Board will also lead and define improvement in safeguarding practice and outcomes and should also ensure that there are effective mechanisms for LSCBs and health and wellbeing boards to raise concerns about the engagement and leadership of the local NHS;

- **clinical commissioning groups (CCGs)** will be the major commissioners of local health services and will be responsible for safeguarding quality assurance through contractual arrangements with all provider organisations. CCGs should employ, or have in place, a contractual agreement to secure the expertise of designated professionals, i.e. designated doctors and nurses for safeguarding children and for looked after children (and designated paediatricians for unexpected deaths in childhood). In some areas there will be more than one CCG per local authority and LSCB area, and CCGs may want to consider developing 'lead' or 'hosting' arrangements for their designated professional team, or a clinical network arrangement. Designated professionals, as clinical experts and strategic leaders, are a vital source of advice to the CCG, the NHS Commissioning Board, the local authority and the LSCB, and of advice and support to other health professionals; and

- all **providers of NHS funded health services** including NHS Trusts, NHS Foundation Trusts and public, voluntary sector, independent sector and social enterprises should identify a named doctor and a named nurse (and a named midwife if the organisation provides maternity services) for safeguarding. In the case of NHS Direct, ambulance trusts and independent providers, this should be a named professional. GP practices should have a lead and deputy lead for safeguarding, who should work closely with named GPs. Named professionals have a key role in promoting good professional practice within their organisation, providing advice and expertise for fellow professionals, and ensuring safeguarding training is in place. They should work closely with their organisation's safeguarding lead, designated professionals and the LSCB.[18]

Police

13. The police are subject to the section 11 duties set out in paragraph 4 of this chapter. Under section 1(8)(h) of the Police Reform and Social Responsibility Act 2011 the police and crime commissioner must hold the Chief Constable to

---

[18]Model job descriptions for designated and named professional roles can be found in the intercollegiate document *Safeguarding Children and Young People: roles and competences for health care staff*.

account for the exercise of the latter's duties in relation to safeguarding children under sections 10 and 11 of the Children Act 2004.

14. All police officers, and other police employees such as Police Community Support Officers, are well placed to identify early when a child's welfare is at risk and when a child may need protection from harm. Children have the right to the full protection offered by the criminal law. In addition to identifying when a child may be a victim of a crime, police officers should be aware of the effect of other incidents which might pose safeguarding risks to children and where officers should pay particular attention. For example, an officer attending a domestic abuse incident should be aware of the effect of such behaviour on any children in the household. Children who are encountered as offenders, or alleged offenders, are entitled to the same safeguards and protection as any other child and due regard should be given to their welfare at all times.

15. The police can hold important information about children who may be suffering, or likely to suffer, significant harm, as well as those who cause such harm. They should always share this information with other organisations where this is necessary to protect children. Similarly, they can expect other organisations to share information to enable the police to carry out their duties. Offences committed against children can be particularly sensitive and usually require the police to work with other organisations such as local authority children's social care. All police forces should have officers trained in child abuse investigation.

16. The police have emergency powers under section 46 of the Children Act 1989 to enter premises and remove a child to ensure their immediate protection. This power can be used if the police have reasonable cause to believe a child is suffering or is likely to suffer significant harm. Police emergency powers can help in emergency situations but should be used only when necessary. Wherever possible, the decision to remove a child from a parent or carer should be made by a court.

Adult social care services

17. Local authorities provide services to adults who are responsible for children who may be in need. These services are subject to the section 11 duties set out in paragraph 4 of this chapter. When staff are providing services to adults they should ask whether there are children in the family and consider whether the children need help or protection from harm. Children may be at greater risk of harm or be in need of additional help in families where the adults have mental health problems, misuse substances or alcohol, are in a violent relationship or have complex needs or have learning difficulties.

18. Adults with parental responsibilities for disabled children have a right to a separate carer's assessment under the Carers (Recognition and Services) Act

1995 and the Carers and Disabled Children Act 2000. The results of this assessment should be taken into account when deciding what services, if any, will be provided under the Children Act 1989.

Housing authorities

19. Housing and homelessness services in local authorities and others at the front line such as environmental health organisations are subject to the section 11 duties set out in paragraph 4 of this chapter. Professionals working in these services may become aware of conditions that could have an adverse impact on children. Under Part 1 of the Housing Act 2004, authorities must take account of the impact of health and safety hazards in housing on vulnerable occupants, including children, when deciding on the action to be taken by landlords to improve conditions. Housing authorities also have an important role to play in safeguarding vulnerable young people, including young people who are pregnant or leaving care.

British Transport Police

20. The British Transport Police (BTP) is subject to the section 11 duties set out in paragraph 4 of this chapter. In its role as the national police for the railways, the BTP can play an important role in safeguarding and promoting the welfare of children, especially in identifying and supporting children who have run away or who are truanting from school.

21. The BTP should carry out its duties in accordance with its legislative powers. This includes removing a child to a suitable place using their police protection powers under the Children Act 1989 and the protection of children who are truanting from school using powers under the Crime and Disorder Act 1998. This involves, for example, the appointment of a designated independent officer in the instance of a child taken into police protection.

Prison Service

22. The Prison Service is subject to the section 11 duties set out in paragraph 4 of this chapter. It also has a responsibility to identify prisoners who pose a risk of harm to children. [19] Where an individual has been identified as presenting a risk of harm to children, the relevant prison establishment:

   - should inform the local authority children's social care services of the offender's reception to prison and subsequent transfers and of the release address of the offender;

---

[19] HMP Public Protection Manual http://www.justice.gov.uk/offenders/public-protection-manual.

- should notify the relevant Probation Trust in the case of offenders who have been sentenced to twelve months or more. The police should also be notified of the release address; and [20]

- may prevent or restrict a prisoner's contact with children. Decisions on the level of contact, if any, should be based on a multi-agency risk assessment. The assessment should draw on relevant information held by police, probation, prison and local authority children's social care.[21]

23. A prison is also able to monitor an individual's communication (including letters and telephone calls) to protect children where proportionate and necessary to the risk presented.

24. Governors/Directors of women's establishments which have Mother and Baby Units should ensure that:

- there is at all times a member of staff on duty in the unit who is proficient in child protection, health and safety and first aid/child resuscitation; and

- each baby has a child care plan setting out how the best interests of the child will be maintained and promoted during the child's residence in the unit.

Probation Service

25. Probation Trusts are subject to the section 11 duties set out in paragraph 4 of this chapter. They are primarily responsible for providing reports for courts and working with adult offenders both in the community and in the transition from custody to community to reduce their reoffending. They are, therefore, well placed to identify offenders who pose a risk of harm to children as well as children who may be at heightened risk of involvement in (or exposure to) criminal or anti-social behaviour and of other poor outcomes due to the offending behaviour of their parent/carer(s).

26. Where an adult offender is assessed as presenting a risk of serious harm to children, the offender manager should develop a risk management plan and supervision plan that contains a specific objective to manage and reduce the risk of harm to children.

27. In preparing a sentence plan, offender managers should consider how planned interventions might bear on parental responsibilities and whether the planned interventions could contribute to improved outcomes for children known to be in an existing relationship with the offender.

---

[20] The management of an individual who presents a risk of harm to children will often be through a multidisciplinary Interdepartmental Risk Management Team (IRMT).
[21] Ministry of Justice Chapter 2, Section 2 of HM Prison Service Public Protection Manual.

The secure estate for children

28. Governors, managers and directors of the following secure establishments are subject to the section 11 duties set out in paragraph 4 of this chapter:

    - a secure training centre;

    - a young offender institution;

    - accommodation provided by or on behalf of a local authority for the purpose of restricting the liberty of children and young people;

    - accommodation provided for that purpose under subsection (5) of section 82 of the Children Act 1989; and

    - such other accommodation or descriptions of accommodation as the Secretary of State may by order specify.

29. Each centre holding those aged under 18 should have in place an annually reviewed safeguarding children policy. The policy is designed to promote and safeguard the welfare of children and should cover issues such as child protection, risk of harm, restraint, recruitment and information sharing. A safeguarding children manager should be appointed and will be responsible for implementation of this policy.[22]

Youth Offending Teams

30. Youth Offending Teams (YOTs) are subject to the section 11 duties set out in paragraph 4 of this chapter. YOTs are multi-agency teams responsible for the supervision of children and young people subject to pre-court interventions and statutory court disposals.[23] They are therefore well placed to identify children known to relevant organisations as being most at risk of offending and to undertake work to prevent them offending. YOTs should have a lead officer responsible for ensuring safeguarding is at the forefront of their business.

31. Under section 38 of the Crime and Disorder Act 1998, local authorities must, within the delivery of youth justice services, ensure the 'provision of persons to act as appropriate adults to safeguard the interests of children and young persons detained or questioned by police officers'.

The United Kingdom Border Agency

32. Section 55 of the Borders, Citizenship and Immigration Act 2009 places upon the United Kingdom Border Agency (UKBA) a duty to take account of the need

---

[22] Detailed guidance on the safeguarding children policy, the roles of the safeguarding children manager and the safeguarding children committee, and the role of the establishment in relation to the LSCB can be found in Prison Service Instruction (PSI) 08/2012 'Care and Management of Young People'.

[23] The statutory membership of YOTs is set out in section 39 (5) of the Crime and Disorder Act 1998.

to safeguard and promote the welfare of children in discharging its functions. Statutory guidance *Arrangements to Safeguard and Promote Children's Welfare in the United Kingdom Border Agency* sets out the agency's responsibilities. [24]

Children and Family Court Advisory and Support Service

33. The responsibility of the Children and Family Court Advisory and Support Service (Cafcass), where they are appointed in care and related proceedings specified in section 41(6) of the Children Act 1989, is to safeguard the welfare of individual children who are the subject of those proceedings. It achieves this by providing independent social work advice to the court.[25]

34. Where Cafcass have been appointed in proceedings specified at section 41(6), they have a statutory right to access: (i) records of, or held by, a local authority or an authorised person which were compiled in connection with an application under the Children Act 1989 and which relate to the child in those proceedings; (ii) records of, or held by, a local authority connected with the authority's social services functions in so far as they relate to the child in those proceedings; and (iii) records of, or held by an authorised person, which were compiled in connection with that person's activities and which relate to that child.[26]

35. Where a Cafcass officer has been appointed by the court as a children's guardian and the matter before the court relates to specified proceedings, they should be invited to all formal planning meetings convened by the local authority in respect of the child. This includes statutory reviews of children who are accommodated or looked after, child protection conferences and relevant Adoption Panel meetings.

Armed Services

36. Local authorities have the statutory responsibility for safeguarding and promoting the welfare of the children of service families in the UK.[27] In discharging these responsibilities:

- local authorities should ensure that the Soldiers, Sailors, Airmen, and Families Association Forces Help, the British Forces Social Work

---

[24] UK Border Agency *Arrangements to Safeguard and Promote Children's Welfare in the United Kingdom Border Agency*.

[25] Section 12(1) of the Criminal Justice and Court Services Act 2000 sets out Cafcass's duty to safeguard and promote the welfare of children involved in family proceedings in which their welfare is, or may be, in question.

[26] Section 31(9) CA 1989 defines an "authorised person" as: (a) the National Society for the Prevention of Cruelty to Children and any of its officers; and (b) any person authorised by order of the Secretary of State to bring proceedings under this section and any officer of a body which is so authorised.

[27] When service families or civilians working with the armed forces are based overseas the responsibility for safeguarding and promoting the welfare of their children is vested in the Ministry of Defence.

Service or the Naval Personal and Family Service is made aware of any service child who is the subject of a child protection plan and whose family is about to move overseas; and[28]

- each local authority with a United States base in its area should establish liaison arrangements with the base commander and relevant staff. The requirements of English child welfare legislation should be explained clearly to the US authorities, so that the local authority can fulfil its statutory duties.

Voluntary and private sectors

37. Voluntary organisations and private sector providers play an important role in delivering services to children. They should have the arrangements described in paragraph 4 of this chapter in place in the same way as organisations in the public sector, and need to work effectively with the LSCB. Paid and volunteer staff need to be aware of their responsibilities for safeguarding and promoting the welfare of children, how they should respond to child protection concerns and make a referral to local authority children's social care or the police if necessary.

Faith Organisations

38. Churches, other places of worship and faith-based organisations provide a wide range of activities for children and have an important role in safeguarding children and supporting families. Like other organisations who work with children they need to have appropriate arrangements in place to safeguard and promote the welfare of children, as described in paragraph 4 of this chapter.

---

[28] A single point of contact for British Forces Social Work Service will be introduced in late 2013.

Chapter 3: Local Safeguarding Children Boards

Section 13 of the Children Act 2004 requires each local authority to establish a Local Safeguarding Children Board (LSCB) for their area and specifies the organisations and individuals (other than the local authority) that should be represented on LSCBs.

Statutory objectives and functions of LSCBs

1. An LSCB must be established for every local authority area. The LSCB has a range of roles and statutory functions including developing local safeguarding policy and procedures and scrutinising local arrangements. The statutory objectives and functions of the LSCB are described in the two boxes below/over.

Statutory objectives and functions of LSCBs

Section 14 of the Children Act 2004 sets out the objectives of LSCBs, which are:

(a) to coordinate what is done by each person or body represented on the Board for the purposes of safeguarding and promoting the welfare of children in the area; and

(b) to ensure the effectiveness of what is done by each such person or body for those purposes.

Regulation 5 of the Local Safeguarding Children Boards Regulations 2006 sets out that the functions of the LSCB, in relation to the above objectives under section 14 of the Children Act 2004, are as follows:

1(a) developing policies and procedures for safeguarding and promoting the welfare of children in the area of the authority, including policies and procedures in relation to:

(i) the action to be taken where there are concerns about a child's safety or welfare, including thresholds for intervention;

(ii) training of persons who work with children or in services affecting the safety and welfare of children;

(iii) recruitment and supervision of persons who work with children;

(iv) investigation of allegations concerning persons who work with children;

(v) safety and welfare of children who are privately fostered;

(vi) cooperation with neighbouring children's services authorities and their Board partners;

(b) communicating to persons and bodies in the area of the authority the need to safeguard and promote the welfare of children, raising their awareness of how this can best be done and encouraging them to do so;

(c) monitoring and evaluating the effectiveness of what is done by the authority and their Board partners individually and collectively to safeguard and promote the welfare of children and advising them on ways to improve;

(d) participating in the planning of services for children in the area of the authority; and

(e) undertaking reviews of serious cases and advising the authority and their Board partners on lessons to be learned.

Regulation 5 (2) which relates to the LSCB Serious Case Reviews function and regulation 6 which relates to the LSCB Child Death functions are covered in chapter 4 of this guidance.

Regulation 5 (3) provides that an LSCB may also engage in any other activity that facilitates, or is conducive to, the achievement of its objectives.

2. In order to fulfil its statutory function under regulation 5 an LSCB should use data and, as a minimum, should:

- assess the effectiveness of the help being provided to children and families, including early help;

- assess whether LSCB partners are fulfilling their statutory obligations set out in chapter 2 of this guidance;

- quality assure practice, including through joint audits of case files involving practitioners and identifying lessons to be learned; and

- monitor and evaluate the effectiveness of training, including multi-agency training, to safeguard and promote the welfare of children. [29,30]

3. LSCBs do not commission or deliver direct frontline services though they may provide training. While LSCBs do not have the power to direct other organisations they do have a role in making clear where improvement is needed. Each Board partner retains their own existing line of accountability for safeguarding.

LSCB membership

4. LSCB membership is set out in the box on page 61.

---

[29] The Children's Safeguarding Performance Information Framework provides a mechanism to help do this by setting out some of the questions a LSCB should consider. Download the framework from DfE.

[30] Research has shown that multi-agency training in particular is useful and valued by professionals in developing a shared understanding of child protection and decision making. Carpenter et al (2009). *The Organisation, Outcomes and Costs of Inter-agency Training to safeguard and promote the welfare of children*. London: Department for Children, Schools and Families.

Statutory Board partners and relevant persons and bodies

Section 13 of the Children Act 2004, read with regulation 3 of the LSCB Regulations, as amended, sets out that an LSCB must include at least one representative of the local authority and each of the other Board partners set out below (although two or more Board partners may be represented by the same person). Board partners who must be included in the LSCB are:

- district councils in local government areas which have them;

- the chief officer of police;

- the Local Probation Trust;

- the Youth Offending Team;

- the NHS Commissioning Board and clinical commissioning groups;

- NHS Trusts and NHS Foundation Trusts all or most of whose hospitals, establishments and facilities are situated in the local authority area;

- Cafcass;

- the governor or director of any secure training centre in the area of the authority; and

- the governor or director of any prison in the area of the authority which ordinarily detains children.

The Apprenticeships, Skills, Children and Learning Act 2009 amended sections 13 and 14 of the Children Act 2004 and provided that the local authority must take reasonable steps to ensure that the LSCB includes two lay members representing the local community.

Section 13(4) of the Children Act 2004, as amended, provides that the local authority must take reasonable steps to ensure the LSCB includes representatives of relevant persons and bodies of such descriptions as may be prescribed. Regulation 3A of the LSCB Regulations prescribes the following persons and bodies:

- the governing body of a maintained school;

- the proprietor of a non-maintained special school;

- the proprietor of a city technology college, a city college for the technology of the arts or an Academy; and

- the governing body of a further education institution the main site of which is situated in the authority's area.

5. All schools (including independent schools, Academies and free schools) have duties in relation to safeguarding children and promoting their welfare and these are covered in chapter 2. Local authorities must take reasonable steps to ensure that the LSCB includes representatives from of all types of school in their area listed at regulation 3A of the LSCB Regulations. A system of representation should be identified to enable all schools to receive information and feed back comments to their representatives on the LSCB.

6. The LSCB should work with the Local Family Justice Board. They should also work with the health and wellbeing board, informing and drawing on the Joint Strategic Needs Assessment.

7. In exceptional circumstances an LSCB can cover more than one local authority. Where boundaries between LSCBs and their partner organisations are not coterminous, such as with health organisations and police authorities, LSCBs should collaborate as necessary on establishing common policies and procedures and joint ways of working.

8. Members of an LSCB should be people with a strategic role in relation to safeguarding and promoting the welfare of children within their organisation. They should be able to:

    ▪ speak for their organisation with authority;
    ▪ commit their organisation on policy and practice matters; and
    ▪ hold their own organisation to account and hold others to account.

9. The LSCB should either include on its Board, or be able to draw on appropriate expertise and advice from, frontline professionals from all the relevant sectors. This includes a designated doctor and nurse, the Director of Public Health, Principal Child and Family Social Worker and the voluntary and community sector.

10. Lay members will operate as full members of the LSCB, participating as appropriate on the Board itself and on relevant committees. Lay members should help to make links between the LSCB and community groups, support stronger public engagement in local child safety issues and an improved public understanding of the LSCB's child protection work. A local authority may pay lay members.

11. The Lead Member for Children should be a participating observer of the LSCB. In practice this means routinely attending meetings as an observer and receiving all its written reports.

LSCB Chair, accountability and resourcing

12. In order to provide effective scrutiny, the LSCB should be independent. It should not be subordinate to, nor subsumed within, other local structures.

13. Every LSCB should have an independent chair who can hold all agencies to account.

14. It is the responsibility of the Chief Executive (Head of Paid Service) to appoint or remove the LSCB chair with the agreement of a panel including LSCB partners and lay members. The Chief Executive, drawing on other LSCB partners and, where appropriate, the Lead Member will hold the Chair to account for the effective working of the LSCB.

15. The LSCB Chair should work closely with all LSCB partners and particularly with the Director of Children's Services. The Director of Children's Services has the responsibility within the local authority, under section 18 of the Children Act 2004, for improving outcomes for children, local authority children's social care functions and local cooperation arrangements for children's services.[31]

16. The Chair must publish an annual report on the effectiveness of child safeguarding and promoting the welfare of children in the local area.[32] The annual report should be published in relation to the preceding financial year and should fit with local agencies' planning, commissioning and budget cycles. The report should be submitted to the Chief Executive, Leader of the Council, the local police and crime commissioner and the Chair of the health and wellbeing board.

17. The report should provide a rigorous and transparent assessment of the performance and effectiveness of local services. It should identify areas of weakness, the causes of those weaknesses and the action being taken to address them as well as other proposals for action. The report should include lessons from reviews undertaken within the reporting period (see chapters 4 and 5).

18. The report should also list the contributions made to the LSCB by partner agencies and details of what the LSCB has spent, including on Child Death Reviews, Serious Case Reviews and other specific expenditure such as learning events or training. All LSCB member organisations have an obligation to provide LSCBs with reliable resources (including finance) that enable the LSCB to be strong and effective. Members should share the financial responsibility for the LSCB in such a way that a disproportionate burden does not fall on a small number of partner agencies.

---

[31] Department for Education statutory guidance on *The roles and responsibilities of the Director of Children's Services and Lead Member for Children's Services* which expands on this role.

[32] This is a statutory requirement under section 14A of the Children Act 2004.

19. All LSCB Chairs should have access to training and development opportunities, including peer networking. They should also have an LSCB business manager and other discrete support as is necessary for them, and the LSCB, to perform effectively.

Information sharing

20. Chapter 1 sets out how effective sharing of information between professionals and local agencies is essential for effective service provision. Every LSCB should play a strong role in supporting information sharing between and within organisations and addressing any barriers to information sharing. This should include ensuring that a culture of information sharing is developed and supported as necessary by multi-agency training.

21. In addition, the LSCB can require a person or body to comply with a request for information.[33] This can only take place where the information requested is for the purpose of enabling or assisting the LSCB to perform its functions. Any request for information about individuals must be necessary and proportionate to the reasons for the request. LSCBs should be mindful of the burden of requests and should explain why the information is needed.

---

[33] Section 14B of the Children Act 2004 which was inserted by section 8 of the Children, Schools and Families Act 2010.

Chapter 4: Learning and improvement framework

1. Professionals and organisations protecting children need to reflect on the quality of their services and learn from their own practice and that of others. Good practice should be shared so that there is a growing understanding of what works well. Conversely, when things go wrong there needs to be a rigorous, objective analysis of what happened and why, so that important lessons can be learnt and services improved to reduce the risk of future harm to children.

2. These processes should be transparent, with findings of reviews shared publicly. The findings are not only important for the professionals involved locally in cases. Everyone across the country has an interest in understanding both what works well and also why things can go wrong.

3. Local Safeguarding Children Boards (LSCBs) should maintain a local learning and improvement framework which is shared across local organisations who work with children and families. This framework should enable organisations to be clear about their responsibilities, to learn from experience and improve services as a result.

4. Each local framework should support the work of the LSCB and their partners so that:

   - reviews are conducted regularly, not only on cases which meet statutory criteria, but also on other cases which can provide useful insights into the way organisations are working together to safeguard and protect the welfare of children;

   - reviews look at what happened in a case, and why, and what action will be taken to learn from the review findings;

   - action results in lasting improvements to services which safeguard and promote the welfare of children and help protect them from harm; and

   - there is transparency about the issues arising from individual cases and the actions which organisations are taking in response to them, including sharing the final reports of Serious Case Reviews (SCRs) with the public.

5. The local framework should cover the full range of reviews and audits which are aimed at driving improvements to safeguard and promote the welfare of children. Some of these reviews (i.e. SCRs and child death reviews) are required under legislation. It is important that LSCBs understand the criteria for determining whether a statutory review is required and always conduct those reviews when necessary.

6. LSCBs should also conduct reviews of cases which do not meet the criteria for an SCR, but which can provide valuable lessons about how organisations are working together to safeguard and promote the welfare of children. Although not required by statute these reviews are important for highlighting good

practice as well as identifying improvements which need to be made to local services. Such reviews may be conducted either by a single organisation or by a number of organisations working together. LSCBs should follow the principles in this guidance when conducting these reviews.

7. Reviews are not ends in themselves. The purpose of these reviews is to identify improvements which are needed and to consolidate good practice. LSCBs and their partner organisations should translate the findings from reviews into programmes of action which lead to sustainable improvements and the prevention of death, serious injury or harm to children.

8. The different types of review include:

   - Serious Case Review (see page 69): for every case where abuse or neglect is known or suspected and **either**:
     - a child dies; or
     - a child is seriously harmed and there are concerns about how organisations or professionals worked together to safeguard the child;
   - child death review (see Chapter 5): a review of all child deaths up to the age of 18;
   - review of a child protection incident which falls below the threshold for an SCR; and
   - review or audit of practice in one or more agencies.

Principles for learning and improvement

9. The following principles should be applied by LSCBs and their partner organisations to all reviews:

   - there should be a culture of continuous **learning and improvement** across the organisations that work together to safeguard and promote the welfare of children, identifying opportunities to draw on what works and promote good practice;
   - the approach taken to reviews should be **proportionate** according to the scale and level of complexity of the issues being examined;
   - reviews of serious cases should be led by individuals who are **independent** of the case under review and of the organisations whose actions are being reviewed;
   - professionals should be involved fully in reviews and invited to contribute their perspectives without fear of being blamed for actions they took in good faith;
   - families, including surviving children, should be invited to contribute to reviews. They should understand how they are going to be involved and their expectations should be managed appropriately and sensitively.

This is important for ensuring that the child is at the centre of the process;[34]

- final reports of SCRs **must be published,** including the LSCB's response to the review findings, in order to achieve **transparency.** The impact of SCRs and other reviews on improving services to children and families and on reducing the incidence of deaths or serious harm to children must also be described in LSCB annual reports and will inform inspections; and

- improvement must be sustained through regular monitoring and follow up so that the findings from these reviews make a real impact on improving outcomes for children.

10. SCRs and other case reviews should be conducted in a way which:

- recognises the complex circumstances in which professionals work together to safeguard children;

- seeks to understand precisely who did what and the underlying reasons that led individuals and organisations to act as they did;

- seeks to understand practice from the viewpoint of the individuals and organisations involved at the time rather than using hindsight;

- is transparent about the way data is collected and analysed; and

- makes use of relevant research and case evidence to inform the findings.

11. LSCBs may use any learning model which is consistent with the principles in this guidance, including the systems methodology recommended by Professor Munro.[35]

---

[34] British Association for the Study and Prevention of Child Abuse and Neglect in Family involvement in case reviews, BASPCAN, further information on involving families in reviews.
[35] Department for Education The Munro Review of Child Protection: Final Report: A Child Centred System, Cm 8062, May 2011 .

Serious Case Reviews

> Regulation 5 of the Local Safeguarding Children Boards Regulations 2006 sets out the functions of LSCBs. This includes the requirement for LSCBs to undertake reviews of serious cases in specified circumstances. Regulation 5(1) (e) and (2) set out an LSCB's function in relation to serious case reviews, namely:
>
> 5 (1) (e) undertaking reviews of serious cases and advising the authority and their Board partners on lessons to be learned.
>
> (2) For the purposes of paragraph (1) (e) a serious case is one where:
>
> (a) abuse or neglect of a child is known or suspected; and
>
> (b) either — (i) the child has died; or (ii) the child has been seriously harmed and there is cause for concern as to the way in which the authority, their Board partners or other relevant persons have worked together to safeguard the child.

12. Cases which meet one of these criteria (i.e. regulation 5(2)(a) and (b)(i) or 5 (2)(a) and (b)(ii) above) **must always** trigger an SCR. In addition, even if one of these criteria are not met an SCR **should always** be carried out when a child dies in custody, in police custody, on remand or following sentencing, in a Young Offender Institution, in a secure training centre or a secure children's home, or where the child was detained under the Mental Capacity Act 2005. Regulation 5(2)(b)(i) includes cases where a child died by suspected suicide.

13. Where a case is being considered under regulation 5(2)(b)(ii), unless it is clear that there are no concerns about inter-agency working, the LSCB **must** commission an SCR. The final decision on whether to conduct the SCR rests with the LSCB Chair. If an SCR is not required because the criteria in regulation 5(2) are not met, the LSCB may still decide to commission an SCR or they may choose to commission an alternative form of case review.

14. LSCBs should consider conducting reviews on cases which do not meet the SCR criteria. They will also want to review instances of good practice and consider how these can be shared and embedded. LSCBs are free to decide how best to conduct these reviews. The LSCB should oversee implementation of actions resulting from these reviews and reflect on progress in its annual report.

National panel of independent experts on Serious Case Reviews

15. From 2013 there will be a national panel of independent experts to advise LSCBs about the initiation and publication of SCRs. The role of the panel will be to support LSCBs in ensuring that appropriate action is taken to learn from serious incidents in all cases where the statutory SCR criteria are met and to ensure that those lessons are shared through publication of final SCR reports. The panel will also report to the Government their views of how the SCR system is working.

16. The panel's remit will include advising LSCBs about:

   - application of the SCR criteria;
   - appointment of reviewers; and
   - publication of SCR reports.

17. LSCBs should have regard to the panel's advice when deciding whether or not to initiate an SCR, when appointing reviewers and when considering publication of SCR reports. LSCB Chairs and LSCB members should comply with requests from the panel as far as possible, including requests for information such as copies of SCR reports and invitations to attend meetings. [36]

18. The text which follows provides a checklist for LSCBs on how to manage the SCR process.

---

[36] In doing so LSCBs will be exercising their powers under regulation 5(3) of the Local Safeguarding Children Boards Regulations 2006 which states that 'an LSCB may also engage in any other activity that facilitates, or is conducive to, the achievement of its objective'.

Serious Case Review checklist

Decisions whether to initiate an SCR

The LSCB for the area in which the child is normally resident must decide whether an incident notified to them meets the criteria for an SCR. This decision should normally be made within one month of notification of the incident. The final decision rests with the Chair of the LSCB. The Chair may seek peer challenge from another LSCB Chair when considering this decision and also at other stages in the SCR process.

The LSCB should let Ofsted and the national panel of independent experts know their decision.

If the LSCB decides not to initiate an SCR, their decision may be subject to scrutiny by the national panel. The LSCB should provide information to the panel on request to inform its deliberations and the LSCB Chair should be prepared to attend in person to give evidence to the panel.

Appointing reviewers

The LSCB should appoint one or more suitable individuals to lead the SCR who have demonstrated that they are qualified to conduct reviews using the approach set out in this guidance. The lead reviewer should be independent of the LSCB and the organisations involved in the case. The LSCB should provide the national panel of independent experts with the name(s) of the individual(s) they appoint to conduct the SCR. The LSCB should consider carefully any advice from the independent expert panel about appointment of reviewers.

Engagement of organisations

The LSCB should ensure that there is appropriate representation in the review process of professionals and organisations who were involved with the child and family. The priority should be to engage organisations in a way which will ensure that important factors in the case can be identified and appropriate action taken to make improvements. The LSCB may decide as part of the SCR to ask each relevant organisation to provide information in writing about its involvement with the child who is the subject of the review.

Timescale for SCR completion

The LSCB should aim for completion of an SCR within six months of initiating it. If this is not possible (for example, because of potential prejudice to related court proceedings), every effort should be made while the SCR is in progress to: (i) capture points from the case about improvements needed; and (ii) take corrective action.

Agreeing improvement action

The LSCB should oversee the process of agreeing with partners what action they need to take in light of the SCR findings.

Publication of reports

All reviews of cases meeting the SCR criteria should result in a report which is published and readily accessible on the LSCB's website for a minimum of 12 months. Thereafter the report should be made available on request. This is important to support national sharing of lessons learnt and good practice in writing and publishing SCRs. From the very start of the SCR the fact that the report will be published should be taken into consideration. SCR reports should be written in such a way that publication will not be likely to harm the welfare of any children or vulnerable adults involved in the case.

Final SCR reports should:

- provide a sound analysis of what happened in the case, and why, and what needs to happen in order to reduce the risk of recurrence;

- be written in plain English and in a way that can be easily understood by professionals and the public alike; and

- be suitable for publication without needing to be amended or redacted.

LSCBs should publish, either as part of the SCR report or in a separate document, information about: actions which have already been taken in response to the review findings; the impact these actions have had on improving services; and what more will be done.

When compiling and preparing to publish reports, LSCBs should consider carefully how best to manage the impact of publication on children, family members and others affected by the case. LSCBs must comply with the Data Protection Act 1998 in relation to SCRs, including when compiling or publishing the report, and must comply also with any other restrictions on publication of information, such as court orders.

LSCBs should send copies of all SCR reports to the national panel of independent experts at least one week before publication. If an LSCB considers that an SCR report should not be published, it should inform the panel which will provide advice to the LSCB. The LSCB should provide all relevant information to the panel on request, to inform its deliberations.

Chapter 5: Child death reviews

The Regulations relating to child death reviews

The Local Safeguarding Children Board (LSCB) functions in relation to child deaths are set out in Regulation 6 of the Local Safeguarding Children Boards Regulations 2006, made under section 14(2) of the Children Act 2004. The LSCB is responsible for:

a) collecting and analysing information about each death with a view to identifying—

> *(i) any case giving rise to the need for a review mentioned in regulation 5(1)(e);*
>
> *(ii) any matters of concern affecting the safety and welfare of children in the area of the authority;*
>
> *(iii) any wider public health or safety concerns arising from a particular death or from a pattern of deaths in that area; and*

(b) putting in place procedures for ensuring that there is a coordinated response by the authority, their Board partners and other relevant persons to an unexpected death.

1. Each death of a child is a tragedy and enquiries should keep an appropriate balance between forensic and medical requirements and supporting the family at a difficult time. Professionals supporting parents and family members should assure them that the objective of the child death review process is not to allocate blame, but to learn lessons. The child death review process will help to prevent further such child deaths.[37]

2. The responsibility for determining the cause of death rests with the coroner or the doctor who signs the medical certificate of the cause of death (and therefore is not the responsibility of the Child Death Overview Panel (CDOP)).

Responsibilities of Local Safeguarding Children Boards (LSCBs)

3. The LSCB is responsible for ensuring that a review of each death of a child normally resident in the LSCB's area is undertaken by a CDOP. The CDOP will have a fixed core membership drawn from organisations represented on the LSCB with flexibility to co-opt other relevant professionals to discuss certain types of death as and when appropriate. The CDOP should include a professional from public health as well as child health. It should be chaired by

---

[37] Department for Education leaflet that can be given to parents, carers and family members to explain the child death review process.

the LSCB Chair's representative. That individual should not be involved directly in providing services to children and families in the area. One or more LSCBs can choose to share a CDOP. CDOPs responsible for reviewing deaths from larger populations are better able to identify significant recurrent contributory factors.

4. LSCBs should be informed of the deaths of all children normally resident in their geographical area. The LSCB Chair should decide who will be the designated person to whom the death notification and other data on each death should be sent.[38] LSCBs should use sources available, such as professional contacts or the media, to find out about cases when a child who is normally resident in their area dies abroad. The LSCB should inform the CDOP of such cases so that the deaths of these children can be reviewed.

5. In cases where organisations in more than one LSCB area have known about or have had contact with the child, lead responsibility should sit with the LSCB for the area in which the child was normally resident at the time of death. Other LSCBs or local organisations which have had involvement in the case should cooperate in jointly planning and undertaking the child death review. In the case of a looked after child, the LSCB for the area of the local authority looking after the child should exercise lead responsibility for conducting the child death review, involving other LSCBs with an interest or whose lead agencies have had involvement as appropriate.

---

[38] Department for Education: list of people designated by the CDOP to receive notifications of child death information.

Specific responsibilities of relevant bodies in relation to child deaths	
Registrars of Births and Deaths (Children and Young Persons Act 2008)	Requirement to supply the LSCB with information which they have about the death of persons under 18 they have registered or re-registered. Notify LSCBs if they issue a *Certificate of No Liability to Register* where it appears that the deceased was or may have been under the age of 18 at the time of death. Requirement to send the information to the appropriate LSCB (the one which covers the sub-district in which the register is kept) no later than seven days from the date of registration.
Coroners (Coroners Rules 1984 (as amended by the Coroners (Amendment) Rules 2008))	Duty to inquire and may require evidence. Duty to inform the LSCB for the area in which the child died within three working days of the fact of an inquest or post mortem. Powers to share information with LSCBs for the purposes of carrying out their functions, including reviewing child deaths and undertaking SCRs.
Registrar General (section 32 of the Children and Young Persons Act 2008)	Power to share child death information with the Secretary of State, including about children who die abroad.

Medical Examiners (Coroners and Justice Act 2009)	It is anticipated that from 2014 Medical Examiners will be required to share information with LSCBs about child deaths that are not investigated by a coroner.
Clinical Commissioning Groups (Health and Social Care Act 2012)	Employ, or have arrangements in place to secure the expertise of, consultant paediatricians whose designated responsibilities are to provide advice on: ▪ commissioning paediatric services from paediatricians with expertise in undertaking enquiries into unexpected deaths in childhood, and from medical investigative services; and ▪ the organisation of such services.

6. A summary of the child death processes to be followed when reviewing all child deaths is set out in Flowchart 6 on page 83. The processes for undertaking a rapid response when a child dies unexpectedly are set out in Flowchart 7 on page 84.

Providing information to the Department for Education

7. Every LSCB is required to supply anonymised information on child deaths to the Department for Education. This is so that the Department can commission research and publish nationally comparable analyses of these deaths.[39]

---

[39]Department for Education detailed guidance on how to supply the information on child deaths.

Specific responsibilities of relevant professionals - When responding rapidly to the unexpected death of a child	
Designated Paediatrician for unexpected deaths in childhood	Ensure that relevant professionals (i.e. coroner, police and local authority social care) are informed of the death; coordinate the team of professionals (involved before and/or after the death) which is convened when a child who dies unexpectedly (accessing professionals from specialist agencies as necessary to support the core team). Convene multi-agency discussions after the initial and final initial post mortem results are available.

Responsibilities of Child Death Overview Panels

8. The functions of the CDOP include:

   - reviewing all child deaths up to the age of 18, excluding those babies who are stillborn and planned terminations of pregnancy carried out within the law;

   - collecting and collating information on each child and seeking relevant information from professionals and, where appropriate, family members;

   - discussing each child's case, and providing relevant information or any specific actions related to individual families to those professionals who are involved directly with the family so that they, in turn, can convey this information in a sensitive manner to the family;

   - determining whether the death was deemed preventable, that is, those deaths in which modifiable factors may have contributed to the death and decide what, if any, actions could be taken to prevent future such deaths;

   - making recommendations to the LSCB or other relevant bodies promptly so that action can be taken to prevent future such deaths where possible;

   - identifying patterns or trends in local data and reporting these to the LSCB;

   - where a suspicion arises that neglect or abuse may have been a factor in the child's death, referring a case back to the LSCB Chair for consideration of whether an SCR is required;

   - agreeing local procedures for responding to unexpected deaths of children; and

   - cooperating with regional and national initiatives – for example, with the National Clinical Outcome Review Programme – to identify lessons on the prevention of child deaths.

9. The aggregated findings from all child deaths should inform local strategic planning, including the local Joint Strategic Needs Assessment, on how to best safeguard and promote the welfare of children in the area. Each CDOP should prepare an annual report of relevant information for the LSCB. This information should in turn inform the LSCB annual report.

Definition of preventable child deaths

10. For the purpose of producing aggregate national data, this guidance defines preventable child deaths as those in which modifiable factors may have contributed to the death. These factors are defined as those which, by means of nationally or locally achievable interventions, could be modified to reduce the risk of future child deaths.

11. In reviewing the death of each child, the CDOP should consider modifiable factors, for example in the family and environment, parenting capacity or service provision, and consider what action could be taken locally and what action could be taken at a regional or national level.

Action by professionals when a child dies unexpectedly

Definition of an unexpected death of a child

12. In this guidance an unexpected death is defined as the death of an infant or child (less than 18 years old) which was not anticipated as a significant possibility for example, 24 hours before the death; or where there was a similarly unexpected collapse or incident leading to or precipitating the events which lead to the death.

13. The designated paediatrician responsible for unexpected deaths in childhood should be consulted where professionals are uncertain about whether the death is unexpected. If in doubt, the processes for unexpected child deaths should be followed until the available evidence enables a different decision to be made.

14. As set out in the Local Safeguarding Children Boards Regulations 2006, LSCBs are responsible for putting in place procedures for ensuring that there is a coordinated response by the authority, their Board partners and other relevant persons to an unexpected death.

15. When a child dies suddenly and unexpectedly, the consultant clinician (in a hospital setting) or the professional confirming the fact of death (if the child is not taken immediately to an Accident and Emergency Department) should inform the local designated paediatrician with responsibility for unexpected child deaths at the same time as informing the coroner and police. The police will begin an investigation into the sudden or unexpected death on behalf of the coroner. A paediatrician should initiate an immediate information sharing and planning discussion between the lead agencies (i.e. health, police and local authority children's social care) to decide what should happen next and who will do it. The joint responsibilities of the professionals involved with the child include:

    - responding quickly to the child's death in accordance with the locally agreed procedures;

    - maintaining a rapid response protocol with all agencies, consistent with the Kennedy principles and current investigative practice from the Association of Chief Police Officers;[40]

---

[40] PJ. Fleming, P.S. Blair, C. Bacon, and P.J. Berry (2000) Sudden Unexpected Death In Infancy. The CESDI SUDI Studies 1993-1996. The Stationery Office London. ISBN 0 11 3222 9988; Royal College of

- making immediate enquiries into and evaluating the reasons for and circumstances of the death, in agreement with the coroner;

- liaising with the coroner and the pathologist;

- undertaking the types of enquiries/investigations that relate to the current responsibilities of their respective organisations;

- collecting information about the death;[41]

- providing support to the bereaved family, referring to specialist bereavement services where necessary and keeping them up to date with information about the child's death; and

- gaining consent early from the family for the examination of their medical notes.

16. If the child dies suddenly or unexpectedly at home or in the community, the child should normally be taken to an Accident and Emergency Department rather than a mortuary. In some cases when a child dies at home or in the community, the police may decide that it is not appropriate to immediately move the child's body, for example because forensic examinations are needed.

17. As soon as possible after arrival at a hospital, the child should be examined by a consultant paediatrician and a detailed history should be taken from the parents or carers. The purpose of obtaining this information is to understand the cause of death and identify anything suspicious about it. In all cases when a child dies in hospital, or is taken to hospital after dying, the hospital should allocate a member of staff to remain with the parents and support them through the process.

18. If the child has died at home or in the community, the lead police investigator and senior health care professional should decide whether there should be a visit to the place where the child died, how soon (ideally within 24 hours) and who should attend. This should almost always take place for cases of sudden infant death.[42] After this visit the senior investigator, visiting health care professional, GP, health visitor or school nurse and local authority children's social care representative should consider whether there is any information to raise concerns that neglect or abuse contributed to the child's death.

19. Where a child dies unexpectedly, all registered providers of healthcare services must notify the Care Quality Commission of the death of a service user – but NHS providers may discharge this duty by notifying the National Health Service Commissioning Board.[43] Where a young person dies at work, the Health and

---

Pathologists and the Royal College of Paediatrics and Child Health (2004) Sudden unexpected death in infancy. A multi-agency protocol for care and investigation. The Report of a working group convened by the Royal College of Pathologists and the Royal College of Paediatrics and Child Health. Royal College of Pathologists and the Royal College of Paediatrics and Child Health, London. www.rcpath.org

[41] See Footnote 32.

[42] See footnote 33.

[43] Regulation 16 of the Care Quality Commission (Registration) Regulations 2009

Safety Executive should be informed. Youth Offending Teams' reviews of safeguarding and public protection incidents (including the deaths of children under their supervision) should also feed into the CDOP child death processes.

20. If there is a criminal investigation, the team of professionals must consult the lead police investigator and the Crown Prosecution Service to ensure that their enquiries do not prejudice any criminal proceedings. If the child dies in custody, there will be an investigation by the Prisons and Probation Ombudsman (or by the Independent Police Complaints Commission in the case of police custody). Organisations who worked with the child will be required to cooperate with that investigation.

Involvement of the coroner and pathologist

21. If a doctor is not able to issue a medical certificate of the cause of death, the lead professional or investigator must report the child's death to the coroner in accordance with a protocol agreed with the local coronial service. The coroner must investigate violent or unnatural death, or death of no known cause, and all deaths where a person is in custody at the time of death. The coroner will then have jurisdiction over the child's body at all times. Unless the death is natural a public inquest will be held.[44]

22. The coroner will order a post mortem examination to be carried out as soon as possible by the most appropriate pathologist available (this may be a paediatric pathologist, forensic pathologist or both) who will perform the examination according to the guidelines and protocols laid down by the Royal College of Pathologists. The designated paediatrician will collate and share information about the circumstances of the child's death with the pathologist in order to inform this process.

23. If the death is unnatural or the cause of death cannot be confirmed, the coroner will hold an inquest. Professionals and organisations who are involved in the child death review process must cooperate with the coroner and provide him/her with a joint report about the circumstances of the child's death. This report should include a review of all medical, local authority social care and educational records on the child. The report should be delivered to the coroner within 28 days of the death unless crucial information is not yet available.

Action after the post mortem

24. Although the results of the post mortem belong to the coroner, it should be possible for the paediatrician, pathologist, and the lead police investigator to discuss the findings as soon as possible, and the coroner should be informed

---

[44] Ministry of Justice guidance for coroners and Local Safeguarding Children Boards on the supply of information concerning the death of children.

immediately of the initial results. If these results suggest evidence of abuse or neglect as a possible cause of death, the paediatrician should inform the police and local authority children's social care immediately. He or she should also inform the LSCB Chair so that they can consider whether the criteria are met for initiating an SCR.

25. Shortly after the initial post mortem results become available, the designated paediatrician for unexpected child deaths should convene a multi-agency case discussion, including all those who knew the family and were involved in investigating the child's death. The professionals should review any further available information, including any that may raise concerns about safeguarding issues. A further multi-agency case discussion should be convened by the designated paediatrician, or a paediatrician acting as their deputy, as soon as the final post mortem result is available. This is in order to share information about the cause of death or factors that may have contributed to the death and to plan future care of the family. The designated paediatrician should arrange for a record of the discussion to be sent to the coroner, to inform the inquest and cause of death, and to the relevant CDOP, to inform the child death review. At the case discussion, it should be agreed how detailed information about the cause of the child's death will be shared, and by whom, with the parents, and who will offer the parents on-going support.

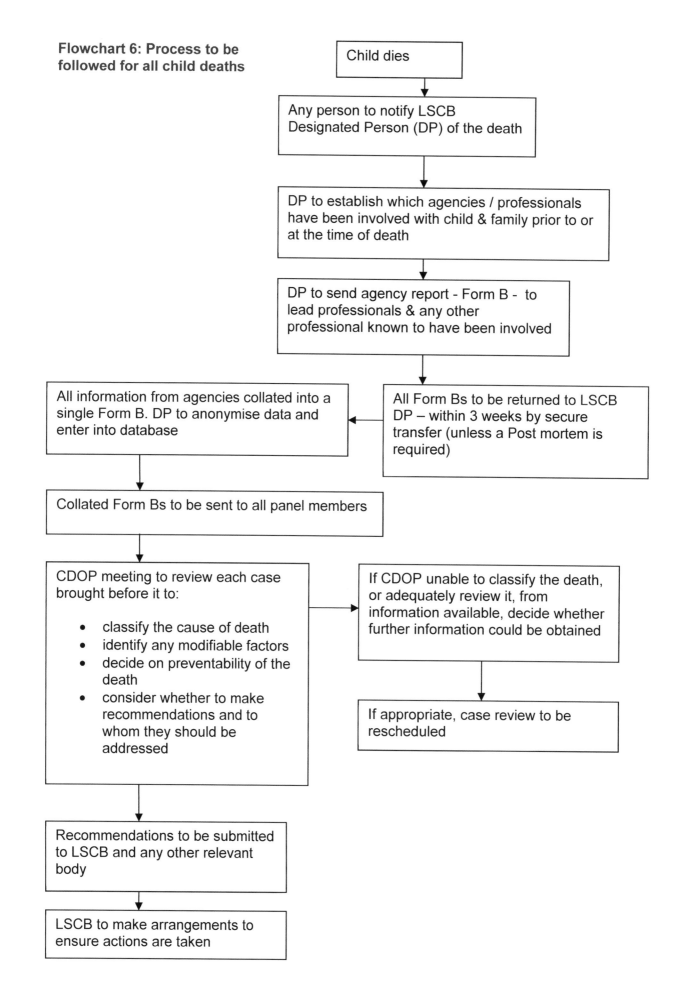

Flowchart 6: Process to be followed for all child deaths

Child dies

↓

Any person to notify LSCB Designated Person (DP) of the death

↓

DP to establish which agencies / professionals have been involved with child & family prior to or at the time of death

↓

DP to send agency report - Form B - to lead professionals & any other professional known to have been involved

↓

All Form Bs to be returned to LSCB DP – within 3 weeks by secure transfer (unless a Post mortem is required)

→

All information from agencies collated into a single Form B. DP to anonymise data and enter into database

↓

Collated Form Bs to be sent to all panel members

↓

CDOP meeting to review each case brought before it to:

- classify the cause of death
- identify any modifiable factors
- decide on preventability of the death
- consider whether to make recommendations and to whom they should be addressed

→

If CDOP unable to classify the death, or adequately review it, from information available, decide whether further information could be obtained

↓

If appropriate, case review to be rescheduled

↓

Recommendations to be submitted to LSCB and any other relevant body

↓

LSCB to make arrangements to ensure actions are taken

83

Flowchart 7: Process for rapid response to the unexpected death of a child

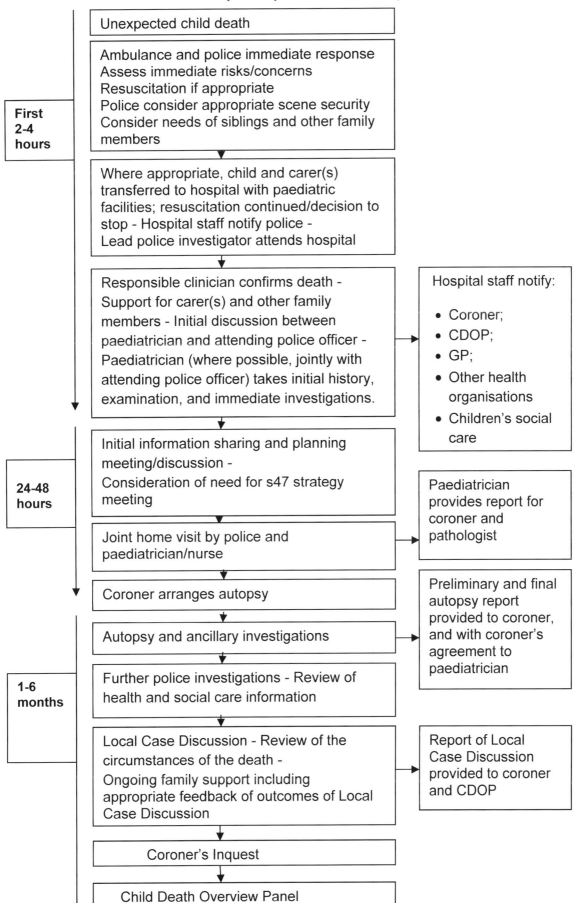

First 2-4 hours

Unexpected child death

Ambulance and police immediate response
Assess immediate risks/concerns
Resuscitation if appropriate
Police consider appropriate scene security
Consider needs of siblings and other family members

Where appropriate, child and carer(s) transferred to hospital with paediatric facilities; resuscitation continued/decision to stop - Hospital staff notify police - Lead police investigator attends hospital

Responsible clinician confirms death - Support for carer(s) and other family members - Initial discussion between paediatrician and attending police officer - Paediatrician (where possible, jointly with attending police officer) takes initial history, examination, and immediate investigations.

Hospital staff notify:
- Coroner;
- CDOP;
- GP;
- Other health organisations
- Children's social care

24-48 hours

Initial information sharing and planning meeting/discussion - Consideration of need for s47 strategy meeting

Joint home visit by police and paediatrician/nurse

Paediatrician provides report for coroner and pathologist

Coroner arranges autopsy

Autopsy and ancillary investigations

Preliminary and final autopsy report provided to coroner, and with coroner's agreement to paediatrician

1-6 months

Further police investigations - Review of health and social care information

Local Case Discussion - Review of the circumstances of the death - Ongoing family support including appropriate feedback of outcomes of Local Case Discussion

Report of Local Case Discussion provided to coroner and CDOP

Coroner's Inquest

Child Death Overview Panel

Appendix A: Glossary

Children	Anyone who has not yet reached their 18th birthday. The fact that a child has reached 16 years of age, is living independently or is in further education, is a member of the armed forces, is in hospital or in custody in the secure estate, does not change his/her status or entitlements to services or protection.
Safeguarding and promoting the welfare of children	Defined for the purposes of this guidance as: • protecting children from maltreatment; • preventing impairment of children's health or development; • ensuring that children are growing up in circumstances consistent with the provision of safe and effective care; and • taking action to enable all children to have the best life chances.
Child protection	Part of safeguarding and promoting welfare. This refers to the activity that is undertaken to protect specific children who are suffering, or are likely to suffer, significant harm.
Abuse	A form of maltreatment of a child. Somebody may abuse or neglect a child by inflicting harm, or by failing to act to prevent harm. Children may be abused in a family or in an institutional or community setting by those known to them or, more rarely, by others (e.g. via the internet). They may be abused by an adult or adults, or another child or children.
Physical abuse	A form of abuse which may involve hitting, shaking, throwing, poisoning, burning or scalding, drowning, suffocating or otherwise causing physical harm to a child. Physical harm may also be caused when a parent or carer fabricates the symptoms of, or deliberately induces, illness in a child.
Emotional abuse	The persistent emotional maltreatment of a child such as to cause severe and persistent adverse effects on the child's emotional development. It may involve conveying to a child that they are worthless or unloved, inadequate, or valued only insofar as they meet the needs of another person. It may include not giving the child opportunities to express their views, deliberately silencing them or 'making fun' of what they say or how they communicate. It may feature age or developmentally inappropriate expectations being imposed on children. These may include interactions that are beyond a child's developmental capability, as well as overprotection and limitation of exploration and learning, or preventing the child participating in normal social interaction. It may involve seeing or hearing the ill-treatment of another. It may involve serious bullying (including cyber bullying), causing children frequently to feel frightened or in danger, or the exploitation or corruption of children. Some level of emotional abuse is

	involved in all types of maltreatment of a child, though it may occur alone.
Sexual abuse	Involves forcing or enticing a child or young person to take part in sexual activities, not necessarily involving a high level of violence, whether or not the child is aware of what is happening. The activities may involve physical contact, including assault by penetration (for example, rape or oral sex) or non-penetrative acts such as masturbation, kissing, rubbing and touching outside of clothing. They may also include non-contact activities, such as involving children in looking at, or in the production of, sexual images, watching sexual activities, encouraging children to behave in sexually inappropriate ways, or grooming a child in preparation for abuse (including via the internet). Sexual abuse is not solely perpetrated by adult males. Women can also commit acts of sexual abuse, as can other children.
Neglect	The persistent failure to meet a child's basic physical and/or psychological needs, likely to result in the serious impairment of the child's health or development. Neglect may occur during pregnancy as a result of maternal substance abuse. Once a child is born, neglect may involve a parent or carer failing to: ▪ provide adequate food, clothing and shelter (including exclusion from home or abandonment); ▪ protect a child from physical and emotional harm or danger; ▪ ensure adequate supervision (including the use of inadequate care-givers); or ▪ ensure access to appropriate medical care or treatment. It may also include neglect of, or unresponsiveness to, a child's basic emotional needs.
Young carers	Are children and young persons under 18 who provide or intend to provide care assistance or support to another family member. They carry out on a regular basis, significant or substantial caring tasks and assume a level of responsibility, which would usually be associated with an adult. The person receiving care is often a parent but can be a sibling, grandparent or other relative who is disabled, has some chronic illness, mental health problem or other condition connected with a need for care support or supervision.

Appendix B: Statutory framework

The legislation relevant to safeguarding and promoting the welfare of children is set out below.

Children Act 2004

Section 10 requires each local authority to make arrangements to promote cooperation between the authority, each of the authority's relevant partners (see Table A) and such other persons or bodies working with children in the local authority's area as the authority considers appropriate. The arrangements are to be made with a view to improving the wellbeing of children in the authority's area – which includes protection from harm or neglect alongside other outcomes.

Section 11 places duties on a range of organisations and individuals (see Table A) to ensure their functions, and any services that they contract out to others, are discharged with regard to the need to safeguard and promote the welfare of children.

Section 13 requires each local authority to establish a Local Safeguarding Children Board (LSCB) for their area and specifies the organisations and individuals (other than the local authority) that the Secretary of State may prescribe in regulations that should be represented on LSCBs.

Section 14 sets out the objectives of LSCBs, which are:

(a) to coordinate what is done by each person or body represented on the Board for the purposes of safeguarding and promoting the welfare of children in the area of the local authority, *and*

(b) to ensure the effectiveness of what is done by each such person or body for the purposes of safeguarding and promoting the welfare of children.

The LSCB Regulations 2006[45] made under sections 13 and 14 set out the functions of LSCBs, which include undertaking reviews of the deaths of all children in their areas and undertaking Serious Case Reviews in certain circumstances.

Under section 55 of the Borders, Citizenship and Immigration Act 2009, the Secretary of State (in practice, the UK Border Agency or 'UKBA') has a duty to ensure that functions relating to immigration and customs are discharged with regard to the need to safeguard and promote the welfare of children.

---

[45] Local Safeguarding Children Boards Regulations 2006 .

Education Act 2002

Section 175 places a duty on local authorities in relation to their education functions, the governing bodies of maintained schools and the governing bodies of further education institutions (which include sixth-form colleges) to exercise their functions with a view to safeguarding and promoting the welfare of children who are either pupils at a school or who are students under 18 years of age attending further education institutions.

The same duty applies to independent schools (which include Academies/free schools) by virtue of regulations made under section 157 of this Act.

Children Act 1989

The Children Act 1989 places a duty on local authorities to promote and safeguard the welfare of children in need in their area.

Section 17(1) of the Children Act 1989 states that it shall be the general duty of every local authority:

> (a) to safeguard and promote the welfare of children within their area who are in need; and

> (b) so far as is consistent with that duty, to promote the upbringing of such children by their families.

by providing a range and level of services appropriate to those children's needs.

Section 17(5) enables the local authority to make arrangements with others to provide services on their behalf and states that every local authority:

> (a) shall facilitate the provision by others (including in particular voluntary organisations) of services which it is a function of the authority to provide by virtue of this section, or section 18, 20, 22A to 22C, 23B to 23D, 24A or 24B; and

> (b) may make such arrangements as they see fit for any person to act on their behalf in the provision of any such service.

Section 17(10) states that a child shall be taken to be in need if:

> (a) the child is unlikely to achieve or maintain, or to have the opportunity of achieving or maintaining, a reasonable standard of health or development without the provision of services by a local authority under Part III of the Children Act 1989;

> (b) the child's health or development is likely to be significantly impaired, or further impaired, without the provision of such services; or

> (c) the child is disabled.

Under section 17, local authorities have responsibility for determining what services should be provided to a child in need. This does not necessarily require local authorities themselves to be the provider of such services.

Section 27 of the Children Act 1989 makes provision for cooperation between local authorities, local authority housing services and health bodies. Where it appears to a local authority that any authority or body mentioned in section 27(3) could, by taking any specified action, help in the exercise of any of their functions under Part 3, they may request the help of that other authority or body, specifying the action in question. An authority or body whose help is so requested shall comply with the request if it is compatible with their own statutory or other duties and obligations and does not unduly prejudice the discharge of any of their functions. The authorities are:

(a) any local authority;

(b) any local housing authority;

(c) any Local Health Board, Special Health Authority, Primary Care Trust, (National Health Service Trust or NHS Foundation Trust; and

d) any person authorised by the Secretary of State for the purpose of section 27.

Section 47(1) of the Children Act 1989 states that:

Where a local authority:

(a) are informed that a child who lives, or is found, in their area (i) is the subject of a emergency protection order, or (ii) is in police protection; and

(b) have reasonable cause to suspect that a child who lives, or is found, in their area is suffering, or is likely to suffer, significant harm:

the authority shall make, or cause to be made, such enquires as they consider necessary to enable them to decide whether they should take any action to safeguard and promote the child's welfare.

Section 53 of the Children Act 2004 amends both section 17 and section 47 of the Children Act 1989, to require in each case that before determining what services to provide or what action to take, the local authority shall, so far as is reasonably practicable and consistent with the child's welfare:

(a) ascertain the child's wishes and feelings regarding the provision of those services or the action to be taken; and

(b) give due consideration (with regard to the child's age and understanding) to such wishes and feelings of the child as they have been able to ascertain.

Emergency protection powers

The court may make an emergency protection order under section 44 of the Children Act 1989, if it is satisfied that there is reasonable cause to believe that a child is likely to suffer significant harm if the child:

- is not removed to different accommodation provided by the applicant; or
- does not remain in the place in which the child is then being accommodated.

Where the applicant is the local authority, an emergency protection order may also be made if enquires (for example, made under section 47) are being frustrated by access to the child being unreasonably refused to a person authorised to seek access, and the applicant has reasonable cause to believe that access is needed as a matter of urgency.

An emergency protection order gives authority to remove a child, and place the child under the protection of the applicant.

Exclusion requirement

The court may include an exclusion requirement in an interim care order or emergency protection order (section 38A and 44A of the Children Act 1989). This allows a perpetrator to be removed from the home instead of having to remove the child. The court must be satisfied that:

- there is reasonable cause to believe that if the person is excluded from the home in which the child lives, the child will cease to suffer, or cease to be likely to suffer, significant harm, or that enquiries will cease to be frustrated; and
- another person living in the home is able and willing to give the child the care that it would be reasonable to expect a parent to give, and consents to the exclusion requirement.

Police protection powers

Under section 46 of the Children Act 1989, where a police officer has reasonable cause to believe that a child could otherwise be likely to suffer significant harm, the officer may:

- remove the child to suitable accommodation; or
- take reasonable steps to ensure that the child's removal from any hospital, or other place in which the child is then being accommodated is prevented.

No child may be kept in police protection for more than 72 hours.

Police Reform and Social Responsibility Act 2011

Section 1(8)(h) requires the police and crime commissioner to hold the chief constable to account for the exercise of the latter's duties in relation to safeguarding children under section 10 and 11 of the Children Act 2004.

Childcare Act 2006

Section 40 requires early years providers to comply with the welfare requirements of the Early Years Foundation Stage.

Crime and Disorder Act 1998

Section 38 requires local authorities, within the delivery of youth justice services, to ensure the provision of persons to act as appropriate adults to safeguard the interests of children and young persons detained or questioned by police officers.

Housing Act 1996

Section 213A of the Housing Act 1996 (inserted by section 12 of the Homelessness Act 2002), housing authorities are required to refer to adult social care services homeless persons with dependent children who are ineligible for homelessness assistance, or are intentionally homeless, or may be threatened with homelessness intentionally, as long as the person consents. If homelessness persists, any child in the family could be in need. In such cases, if social services decide the child's needs would be best met by helping the family to obtain accommodation, they can ask the housing authority for reasonable advice and assistance in this, and the housing authority must give reasonable advice and assistance.

Table A: Bodies and individuals covered by key duties

Body	CA 2004 Section 10 - duty to cooperate	CA 2004 Section 11 - duty to safeguard & promote welfare	Ed Act 2002 Section 175 - duty to safeguard & promote welfare and regulations	CA 2004 Section 13 - statutory partners in LSCBs	CA 1989 Section 27 - help with children in need	CA 1989 Section 47 - help with enquiries about significant harm
Local Authorities and District councils	X	X	In relation to their education functions.	X	X	X
Local policing body	X	X				X
Chief officer of police	X	X		X		X
Local probation board	X	X		X		
SoS re probation services' functions under s2 and 3 of the Offender Management Act (OMA) 2007	X	X		X		
Providers of probation services required under s3(2) OMA 2007 to act as relevant partner of a local authority	X	X		X		
British Transport Police		X				
United Kingdom Border Agency		x under section 55 of the Borders, Citizenship and Immigration Act 2009				
Prison or secure training centre		X		X (which ordinarily detains children)		

Youth offending services	X	X		X		
NHS Commissioning Board	X	X		X	X	X
Clinical commissioning groups	X	X		X	X	X
NHS Trusts and NHS Foundation Trusts		X		X	X	X
Cafcass				X		
Maintained schools	X (includes non-maintained special schools)		X			
FE colleges	X		X			
Independent schools	X		X Via regulations made under section 157 of the Education Act 2002			
Academies and Free Schools	X		X Via regulations made under section 157 of the Education Act 2002			
Contracted services including those provided by voluntary organisations		X				

Appendix C: Further sources of information

Supplementary guidance on particular safeguarding issues

Department for Education guidance

Safeguarding children who may have been trafficked

Safeguarding children and young people who may have been affected by gang activity

Safeguarding children from female genital mutilation

Forced marriage

Safeguarding children from abuse linked to faith or belief

Use of reasonable force

Safeguarding children and young people from sexual exploitation

Safeguarding Children in whom illness is fabricated or induced

Preventing and tackling bullying

Safeguarding children and safer recruitment in education

Information sharing

Recruiting safely: Safer recruitment guidance helping to keep children and young people safe

Safeguarding Disabled Children: Practice guidance

Department of Health / Department for Education: National Service Framework for Children, Young People and Maternity Services

DfE: What to do if you're worried a child is being abused

Guidance issued by other government departments and agencies

Foreign and Commonwealth Office / Home Office: Forced marriage

Ministry of Justice: Guidance on forced marriage

Home Office: What is domestic violence?

Department of Health: The Framework for the Assessment of Children in Need and their Families 2000: Practice guidance

Department of Health: Responding to domestic abuse: A handbook for health professionals

NHS National Treatment Agency: Guidance on development of Local Protocols between drug and Alcohol Treatment Services and Local Safeguarding and Family Services

Home Office: Guidance on teenage relationship abuse

Youth Justice Board: Guidance on people who present a risk to children

Department of Health: Violence against Women and Children

UK Border Agency: Arrangements to Safeguard and Promote Children's Welfare in UKBA

Department of Health: Good practice guidance on working with parents with a learning disability

Home Office: Circular 16/2005 - Guidance on offences against children

Home Office: Disclosure and Barring Services

Child protection and the Dental Team – an introduction to safeguarding children in dental practice

Ministry of Justice: Multi Agency Public Protection Arrangements guidance

Ministry of Justice: HM Prison Service Public Protection Manual

Ministry of Justice: Probation service guidance on conducting serious further offence reviews Framework.

Missing Children and Adults - a cross Government strategy

Department of Health: Recognised, valued and supported: next steps for the Carers Strategy

Department of Health: Mental Health Act 1983 Code of Practice: Guidance on the visiting of psychiatric patients by children

Guidance issued by external organisations

BAAF: Private fostering

Royal College of Paediatrics and Child Health: Safeguarding Children and Young people: roles and competencies for health care staff - Intercollegiate document, September 2010

General Medical Council: Protecting children and young people - The responsibilities of all doctors

Royal College of Nursing: Looked after children - Knowledge, skills and competences of health care staff (Intercollegiate role framework)

NICE: Guidance on when to suspect child maltreatment

Supplementary guidance to support assessing the needs of children

DfE: What to do if you're worried a child is being abused

DfE: Childhood neglect - Improving outcomes for children

NICE: When to suspect child maltreatment

Supplementary guidance to support the Learning and Improvement Framework

DfE: Training in relation to the child death review processes and Serious Case Reviews

NPIA / ACPO: Guidance on Investigating Child Abuse and Safeguarding Children

Prison and Probation Ombudsman's fatal incidents investigation